D1553275

# GEMBITCH
## Global Adventures

### Sondra Francis

# GEMBITCH: GLOBAL ADVENTURES

Copyright © 2016 by Sondra Francis

All rights reserved. Printed in the United States of America. No part of this publication may be reproduced, stored in a retrieval system, or transmitted, in any form or by any means electronic, mechanical, photocopying, recording, or otherwise, without the prior written permission of the author except in the case of brief quotations embodied in critical articles and reviews.

ISBN 978-0-692-66634-0

Edited by Carleton E. Sheppard

Cover Design: Donna Osborn Clark at

CreationsByDonna@gmail.com

Layout and Interior Design: www.CreationByDonna.com

Published by: Gotrocks Publishing

Manufactured in the United States of America

First Edition

# Acknowledgments

Without the help, encouragement, and editing of Carleton Sheppard, this story never would have been told. Malinda Daniel and Nanci Knott have been great cheerleaders for this project.

This journey depended on my meeting Frederick Pough and Lenard Taylor; without them the adventures would not have happened. I owe my education in gem business politics to Roland Naftule. Many others led the way to open my eyes to discover a very interesting world.

# Table of Contents

# Chapter 1 - HOW I BECAME THE GEMBITCH

December 23, 1971--Queretaro, Mexico

As the winter sun began to dim, brilliant Christmas lights around the zocalo (town square) cast a perfect light on the rainbow of colors flashing from the fire opal. My husband, Steve, and I were in the old colonial city of Queretaro, Mexico, located near fire opal deposits. Local gem dealers had approached us with their treasures. The dealers waited patiently as we viewed each parcel of opal cabochons. These were not the bland blue-white bodied opals mined in Australia; these had yellow and orange and crystal clear body colors. Then there was the spectral display jumping out, hypnotizing me. Carefully, Steve and I sorted through the parcels, selecting the best. A dealer produced a small portable gem scale with two small metal bowls. As the opals were placed in the left bowl, tiny carat weights were added to the right-hand bowl, one by one, until the scale maintained a perfect balance. In well-spoken English the dealer pronounced, "One hundred and twelve carats." He gave us a questioning glance.

Steve replied, "One hundred dollars, U.S."

"Okay, bueno." The dealer took the opals and put them back into a carefully-folded paper designed so the gems would not fall out. Steve took the dollars from his wallet, the exchange took place, we all shook hands. And the dealer continued around the square searching for the few tourists there.

We tried not to appear too excited, so we went down the street to a small café which had the most amazing flan and Mexican coffee. We opened up the paper and examined each stone, thinking we had made a big killing. It wasn't as if we knew what we were going to do with the stones. We weren't going to sell them, nor were we going to set them into jewelry. But we had the goods!

When we planned this Christmas vacation to Mexico, we had started out in Mexico City to see the Anthropology Museum and the art museum with the Diego Riveras, Orozcos, and works by other artists. One day we even went to the horse races. However we soon tired of the big city and took a bus to Queretaro, a capital city with a quiet dignity and modest prosperity. We found a hotel room with a balcony facing the zocalo. Off the tourist path, it was clean and decorated for the Christmas holiday. We had not anticipated that we would meet opal dealers. That was a surprise.

This wasn't our first experience with opals. Steve and I worked in Los Angeles in the '60s. He worked for the County Assessor's office and I taught art and home economics at Gardena High School. We took our vacations over Labor Day weekend and the following week. California Admission Day, September 8, gave us an additional holiday before schools started. We would pack our little teal- colored Volkswagen bug and head up US 395 to the vast solitude of northern Nevada. Ideally our destination was Virgin Valley in Washoe County just south of the Oregon border. The quiet desolation and wide open space provided a sense of healing after leaving the madness of Los Angeles. In L.A. there was always an ambient noise level. Total silence doesn't exist in metropolises. In Virgin Valley only an occasional car drove on the winding two lane road and at sunset the coyotes began their howling hunt. Other than that, total silence. Our visits were in the late 1960s. Few visitors disturbed this barren paradise.

Millennia ago this area was a large evergreen forest and then it was covered by the Great Basin inland sea. Now it is high desert studded with sagebrush. All this sits on a geothermal area studded with hot springs (some very hot) and a few cold sink holes. One part of the landscape features a hot water creek. Once we crossed this creek barefoot and scalded our feet. We never tried that again!

At that time in Virgin Valley there was an abandoned house that once belonged to Basque shepherds. In the 1960s it was on public lands. Adjacent to the house was a stone structure that was next to a natural warm springs pool. Water from the spring was piped into the stone building creating an amazing bath house containing shower heads constantly flowing with an endless supply of perfect shower temperature water. The floor consisted of raised wooden slats. Beneath the slats tiny rattle snakes slept, enjoying the warmth. Fortunately these creatures were docile and never bothered anyone, at least when we visited. Those were the perks!

In L.A. the stars are imbedded in the cement sidewalks; light and air pollution hide the sky. Here, we threw our sleeping bags over a tarp under the Milky Way. (We didn't own a tent.) In the mornings we would pick up our sleeping bags and brush off the tiny scorpions which moved in for warmth in the night. Meals were cooked on a small portable barbeque containing a briquette fire.

The Virgin Valley area of Nevada is sandy. Over the millennia, the silica sand replaced the cells in the wood of the dead forest, creating petrified opalized fossils. One could easily dig in the soft, sandy soil to find bits of the opalized material. Screen was used to sift out the sand, leaving larger pieces to be examined for opal. Part of this opalized area was mined by a private company. They had the best area for finding very gemmy material, but there was plenty of open ground available for rock hounds to dig in. Unfortunately most of this opal material would craze (crack) once it was removed from the soil. Consequently it had little commercial value. But to a rock hound this opal represented priceless treasure.

Across the road from the opal bearing area was a basalt outcropping with a rich gemmy orange carnelian. This material formed in the seams of the basalt and was somewhat flat in shape but it had an even translucence. It was easy to pry out of the basalt, so we added carnelian to our treasures.

As a child I was fascinated with rocks and gems. Like a magpie my eye caught any pretty sparkly thing. I used to pore through the Encyclopedia Britannica looking for all the pictures of gemstones and crystals and my favorite was a large bi-colored tourmaline crystal.

After Steve and I were married we would explore some of the gem material locations around Southern California just like all the other rock hounds. Steve had been on rock hunts with his father. He knew several sites in Southern California where we could pick up crystals and "pretty" rocks. For me this was a new adventure. Even though we collected a lot of rocks I never envisioned a career in the gem business.

We were aware that the Gemological Institute was located on San Vincente Boulevard, not too far from where we lived. We even talked about taking classes there but never carried through with the idea. We lived close to University High School in West Los Angeles where they offered a night class in gem cutting and jewelry making. So we took our bag of rough gem material over there and cut cabochons (rounded, unfaceted stones) and set them in our own handmade silver mountings. My jewelry pieces told me that I could never be a bench jeweler-- this was not a field where I had natural talent. I found jewelry construction tedious and I was never satisfied with my end product.

We had a comfortable life in Los Angeles, but the late sixties were a crazy time with the Manson killings and a restless population in Southwest L.A. One Friday afternoon we were eating an early dinner and six gunshots rang out. We thought the neighbors below us had finally ended their seemingly endless arguments. But after the gunshots the argument below continued. So we looked out the back window into the alley and saw a shooting victim on the ground. Within a few minutes hundreds of people had gathered along with police. The police asked who owned the car with all the bullet holes in it. We sent them to the apartment with the people still yelling and they hesitated to disturb the argument. Steve finally knocked on the neighbor's door and the fight ceased and they came out, examined the car, and then realized that the bullets had also gone into their apartment. The Lalaland craziness began to get to me.

Change is constant in the universe and change came to Los Angeles City Schools in 1970. The city was forced into budget cuts that drastically affected the schools. At the same time the American Federation of Teachers campaigned to unionize the schools. Spring semester some of the teachers went on strike. In Gardena this amounted to about half the faculty striking while half continued to teach, myself included. During this crisis student attendance was optional for those classes still being taught. The first few days of the strike less than half the students stayed away. By the second week almost all of the students came to the classes that were still being taught. The strike ended after a few weeks. I had been teaching there for two and a half years; I was not tenured but I had seniority over the newer hires. The next school year I would have had a job somewhere in Los Angeles City Schools teaching something. But since art and home economics headed the list of classes to be dropped, my position would be lost. One September day in 1970 we moved to Reno, Nevada, expecting a simpler and quieter life.

Steve was hired immediately at the Washoe County Assessor's office. Fall semester, 1972, I started teaching my dream home economics curriculum, a little heavier since I was pregnant. As the baby was due in March, I had to have six weeks of lesson plans ready for the substitute teacher.

I worked until the week before our daughter Sydney was born, took five more weeks off and returned to school. Sydney had a great babysitter who lived a block away from home. Motherhood and teaching seemed very workable in my mind. Fall of 1973 I was back at school, Sydney was receiving great care with a stay-at-home mom, and then the harassment began. Steve, my mother-in-law, and my family began telling me I should stay at home with Sydney. The guilt got to me and at the end of the school year I resigned from my beloved job.

Okay, maybe I can cook, sew and teach child development, but staying home was a dull hopeless prison for me. I became depressed. I had lost my identity, I was Steve Francis's wife, "what's her name" and Sydney's mother. At 34, my life seemed to chill. How long was this sentence to last? After four months I enrolled in the Gemological Institute of America's gemologist course by correspondence. The course included intense lessons in diamonds, then colored stones, gem identification and two one-week classes that had to be taken in Santa Monica at the GIA labs. This took me a couple of years. Meanwhile Steve started his own business as an independent real estate appraiser. I begged him to let me type his appraisals so I could feel somewhat productive.

Other rock hounds had mentioned there was a big gem and mineral show in Tucson, Arizona every February. In 1977 Steve and I went to this legendary show. We stayed at a dude ranch with tennis courts — it was a little bit of work and a lot of vacation. Tucson was a small town then with a western flavor. There were several gem and mineral exhibitors at this time, most of them in the motels skirting the east side of Interstate 10. The Marriott on Broadway housed several higher-end stone dealers. I bought a small parcel of heart-shaped rubies from Leon Ritzler, who eventually would be the first president of the American Gem Trade Association. These Thai rubies were reasonably priced. Every night I would dream of gems. Big excitement!

Growth requires transcendence. One must overcome self-imposed limitations, let go of fear, and jump into the unknown. I didn't wake up one day and think "I want to be a gem dealer." When I decided on my career path I didn't even know there was such a possibility.

In September, 1977, I received my Graduate Gemologist degree, opened up a small office in downtown Reno, and typed real estate appraisals until some gem appraisal work developed. At that time I saw myself as a jewelry appraiser, and I slowly developed a clientele. One meeting totally changed my life. An older man appeared at my office door and said, "I'm Pough" (pronounced "Poe"). I had no idea who he was, but he seemed to think that I should have been fully aware of who he was. "I'm taking a group to Brazil for a gem buying trip," he informed me. And I managed to go.

## Chapter 2 - TIME TO HIT THE AIR

I told Steve about the meeting with Dr. Pough. He gave me a strange look and went to the book case and pulled out a copy of "A Field Guide to Rocks and Minerals" by Frederick H. Pough. "This guy?" Steve asked. "Oh, yeah, that guy." Then I was impressed. Steve and I discussed the trip to Brazil and I decided to stop in Bogota, Colombia before joining the tour in Brazil. Finding an emerald source was my goal. Dr. Pough advised me where to stay in Bogota. Now I could plan this trip that had only seemed like a fantasy before I had met Fred. In my naivete I was jumping into the rabbit hole without thought or hesitation. I was too ignorant to consider a life in gems might have a dark side or could even be dangerous.

Colombia seemed like an obvious choice because there are two principle emerald mines — El Chivor and Muzo. The finest quality Colombian emeralds are generally considered the world's best. The superior quality stones have an intense deep green and are "eye clean," although few are truly flawless under magnification. The inclusions (the internal landscape, also called "flaws") in emeralds can be a good thing-- inclusions from different sources of emeralds indicate the origin of the stone. Inclusions also differentiate natural emeralds from synthetic emeralds.

Before the Spanish conquered Colombia in 1537, the natives actively mined the emeralds and traded them throughout Central America and south into Peru and Bolivia. When the Spanish stole these emeralds from the native inhabitants they did not know the source of the stones. The native miners kept these sources secret. Apparently a child of a miner told the Spanish the location of the El Chivor mine. The Spanish took over the mine and built extensive aquaducts and terraces. After a hundred years the mine appeared to be played out. By then the Muzo mine had been found by the Spanish and the jungle consumed the played-out El Chivor. Today the government controls the emerald mining industry and the distribution of emerald rough. But I was not looking for rough (gems as they come from the earth): I needed faceted gems.

**July 20, 1978--Leaving Reno**

Braniff Airlines offered a good fare to Bogota. Colombia was a reasonable stop on the way to Brazil. Why not? The flight was an overnight venture. Unfortunately it was dark outside and I could not see what we were flying over. The plane was not crowded so I had two wide comfortable leather seats to enjoy for the evening. Those were great days for flying tourist class. Bigger seats and more leg room allowed one to feel well treated. The food and service were excellent. Flying was fun — back then. The flight was due to arrive at 10 a.m. I was too excited to sleep.

**July 21, 1978--Bogota, Colombia**

I arrived on time and proceeded through customs without problems in a modern efficient airport. I took a taxi through a gray modern city to the Tequendama Hotel, recommended by Dr. Pough. Of course, you cannot check into your room at 10 a.m., but they were kind enough to store my bags until my room became available.

International flights seem to be scheduled so the flyer arrives in the morning. This is great, except I felt pretty grimy after an overnight flight. This was the first of many lengthy trips. As time went on the planes became more crowded, the seats were smaller, leg room was shortened, food was worse. One of my irritations on international flights was that women would use the restrooms to primp just before landing. I wish they had separate men's and women's bathrooms. Experience tells me men often have bad aim in these extremely tiny spaces and the floors look suspiciously wet and dirty. Women rarely miss where it counts in these cramped toilets. Right after breakfast women would go into the bathroom for seemingly endless periods of time and come out with bright new makeup and every hair in place. By the time they left the toilets the seat belt sign would come on and the plane would prepare for landing. In a perfect world airlines would provide mirrored makeup areas and leave the mirrors out of the toilet compartments for more efficient use of the toilets.

So there I was. Bogota! At this time Bogota had a reputation as a dangerous city, but this was before the drug wars hit the streets with excessive violence. Then fantasy hit reality for me! What to do? How would I find sources for emeralds? With fuzzy feeling teeth and disheveled hair I wandered the streets. Wide streets and high-rise buildings defined the downtown area. There was a large grassy park area with pre-Columbian stone sculptures. But there were no guys walking the streets with parcels of emeralds, or even fake emeralds, looking for unsuspecting tourists to rip off. Life has its disappointments. I didn't find an emerald source: I had no leads, no addresses, no phone numbers. Reality check! Connections were essential. And I did not fit the stereotype of a gem dealer. But I only allowed two days for this visit, so I looked for other entertainment.

Finally I found a tour that visited coffee plantations and viewed the nearby countryside. Bogota sits on a high plain 8,000 feet above sea level. Most of Colombia sits barely north of the equator with a small portion of the country extending below the equator, so the days and nights are about twelve hours each with little variation through the year. High elevation climate and many sunny days are ideal for growing things, especially coffee. Ample rainfall supports rainforests, creating a luscious landscape. We passed raging streams and impressive waterfalls spewing dingy brackish water. Obviously water pollution went unchecked. I returned to the hotel, ate dinner there and spent a lonely boring night in my room. This was the beginning of a lifestyle with frequent lonely evenings in hotel rooms. Sitting at a bar somewhere was simply out of the question, not my style.

July 22, 1978

After an unproductive first day in Bogota I decided to go to the Gold Museum (Dr. Pough's recommendation). Mistakenly I had thought the Incas dominated pre-Columbian western South America. Not so, the Incan Empire controlled portions of Peru, Bolivia and northern Chile from around A. D. 1200 to 1471. The high plains of

Colombia have been inhabited for 15,000 years. For 2,000 years before the arrival of the conquistadors, the native groups employed rather sophisticated agricultural practices, goldsmithing techniques, stone carving, and fine ceramic production. Mineral-rich Colombia has numerous gold and copper deposits as well as emeralds and quartz.

The Gold Museum is located in a multistoried building. On the top level of the museum is the Gold Room. I entered the room alone, the door closed, the room went dark. I stood there for a minute in total darkness. Slowly, brilliant light of a golden "sunrise" illuminated the display cases. Amulets in the forms of small creatures in gold and carved quartz were suspended in a magical wonderland. It was like a forest of frogs, lizards, butterflies, birds and other creatures creating a sense of reverence of the natural world which dominated the spiritual thinking of the natives. Awestruck, I breathed in this beauty. This was a profound spiritual experience.

Amulets and talismans were universally used by the ancients. The symbolism varied with each community, reflecting their spiritual and religious beliefs. On a later visit I toured the National Museum of Costa Rica. The symbolism used in Costa Rica included versions of flying creatures such as dragonflies and butterflies. Of course there were contacts between the inhabitants of Central America and Colombia. The presence of Colombian emeralds in Central America proves the point. Somehow I had thought of these pre-Columbian cultures as being primitive. The beautiful objects of the gold museum were impressive when I thought about the difficulty of the gold and silver technology of the time.

In 1965 I had been in Taxco, Mexico, an area rich with silver. I found a silversmith who would make a ring for me. As I watched, the silversmith made a simple wax model, placed it in wet sand, burned out the wax with a torch and poured in molten silver (in the space where the wax had been). When the silver was cool the silversmith polished the silver with an electric polishing machine. Into the clean polished setting, he mounted a round smoky quartz gem. All this took about an hour! But that was with twentieth-century technology using gas torches and electrical polishing machines. The ancient Colombian had developed this lost wax technology a thousand or so years before without electricity or gas torches. This process was the same as the Bronze Age technology in the Middle East. Was this a coincidence? Was there an ancient exchange of this technology or do great minds think alike?

I managed to keep busy the rest of the day touring the shops in downtown Bogota. I bought Sydney an 18K gold amulet set with a tiny emerald featuring the Tequendama god. Tequendama, a waterfall as well as the major god, represented the celestial bridge from the earth to the hidden home of the local gods. According to legend, the gods were accessible through certain lakes, oases, and caverns.

I dreaded another evening locked in my hotel room. Since it was my last night in Colombia I wandered out of the hotel and stumbled upon an international trade fair. In 1978 the U.S.A. still had a beef with the "Soviet Eastern Bloc" and this fair was full of Eastern Bloc countries. I wandered around pavilions from Cuba, the USSR, and finally Albania. It was obvious I was a foreigner, probably an American, and the only blond in the place. In certain places I do not blend in with native populations. I wasn't paying much attention to the crowd around me. Suddenly I was surrounded by ten or twelve small children appearing to be under the age of seven. It was kind of scary, I was feeling trapped. Finally I found an escape route and went back to the hotel. Enough evening adventure!

Early the next morning I checked out of the hotel and taxied to the airport. I stood in line and opened my purse to find that my tickets were missing. The purse had outside pockets where the tickets were stored — until the little brats from the Albanian pavilion stole them. And I didn't even know until I was at the airport. At that time a paper ticket was essential to travel even though I had a reservation and a passport. I panicked! On a good day I can "hablo un poco Espanol," but not that day. It was pretty early Sunday morning and no one seemed to speak English at the check-in desk. I made a hysterical call to Steve and, of course, there was no way he could help me from thousands of miles away. I wasted a lot of time trying to get a boarding pass. The clerk had positively decided she did not speak English. Time was passing, the plane was boarding, so finally I was forced to purchase a new ticket. At this point I was expedited through customs and security. I think they wanted me out of there and I was ready to go.

Traveling is a learning experience. And maybe a little fear and caution could be a good thing.

- Lesson One: Beware of groups of children who surround and distract you. These kids may be trained and they may be expert pickpockets. Years later, I would run into another group of kids in the Paris Metro. By then I knew the routine and I made a scene until an adult called them off.

- Lesson Two: Don't carry important documents with you unless absolutely necessary. Find a secure spot inside your purse, or leave them in a safe at the hotel, or figure out how not to carry a purse. (Not carry a purse? — too revolutionary for me.)

- Lesson Three: As a lone woman, be aware, walk with a swagger, assume a look on your face that says you could rip an attacker's face off.

- Lesson Four: Bring a good book or two.

- Lesson Five: Be alert.

- Lesson Six: Arrange contacts for your business before you venture into a foreign country.

# Chapter 3 - ROAD TO RIO

July 23, 1978--Bogota to Rio de Janiero

From a window seat I could see the vast seemingly endless green vistas of the Amazon Basin for hours. Brazil, the third largest country in the world, has a variety of climates and geological features. Besides the Amazon Basin, there are high plateaus, lengthy shorelines bordering the Atlantic, and a variety of forests. Mineral deposits, especially gem minerals, provide the allure to the gem lover. Tourmaline, topaz, beryl (emeralds and aquamarines), spodumene (kunzite), quartz (amethyst, citrine, crystal quartz), sodalite, chrysoberyl (alexandrite), andalusite, and more are mined in Brazil.

One positive legacy of World War II was those individuals who escaped from the horrors of the Third Reich and landed in Brazil. On November 8 and 9, 1938, the Jewish sections of cities throughout Germany felt the anti-Semitic hatred that had been brewing during the rise of Hitler. Windows of Jewish owned businesses were broken; buildings were burned. This event is referred to as "Kristallnacht" (night of broken glass). Jewish men were rounded up and taken to Dachau concentration camp. After this terrible act of violence there were 20,000 orphaned Jewish children. The British government quickly formed "kindertransport" and managed to rescue and bring 10,000 children to England. Many found their way to Brazil and some of them became the people who helped develop the country's incredible gemstone riches.

There was no doubt Dr. Frederick Pough (Fred) was brilliant. He received his B.S. and Ph.D. from Harvard. In the early 1930s he attended the University of Heidelberg in Germany. During the rise of Hitler he was appalled by the anti-Semitism and he took photographs of the many signs excluding Jews from certain places. He left Germany in 1933.

Fred worked with the Manhattan Project during World War II. His assignment was to find particular crystals with piezoelectric properties for the A bomb detonator. Quartz and tourmaline crystals possess the piezoelectric ability.

These crystals conduct electrical charges in a controlled manner. Later in the mid twentieth century synthetic quartz (silicon dioxide) was developed. This synthetic mineral contributed to the development of all the electronic items we use today. The name "Silicon Valley" indicates the importance of these technologies. While he was exploring minerals in Brazil during WWII, he discovered a new mineral, which he named "brazilianite." Brazilianite is a rare stone with a hardness of 5 ½ and it is brittle. It is not used in jewelry.

After the war he worked on the irradiation of gemstones. Irradiation (in a cyclotron) and heating can improve or change the color of some gem materials, but not all gems react to this process. Fred approached the irradiation of gemstones as a scientist. He never considered gemstone treatment as a device for deception. Blue topaz was one extraordinary result of this treatment. Natural blue topaz has a very faint blue color that is not particularly appealing. With irradiation and heat, spectacular blues are the result. Off-colored diamonds were irradiated by Fred, resulting in brilliant yellows, blues, and greens.

The Museum of Natural History in New York hired him as their curator of minerals. The Fred that I got to know had a great sense of humor. He was a liberal political critic. More than anything he was a party boy. He lived a mile away from me in Reno and became a close family friend.

Born in 1906, he was 72 when I met him. About five feet tall, he had boundless energy and walked at terrific speed as though he had somewhere important to go. Every evening began with three shots of vodka, at least, or whatever was the particular beverage of the location. He lived until about six weeks before his one hundredth birthday. How fortunate I was to meet Fred.

Fred and the other tour members were already in Rio. I took a taxi to the hotel and met the group for dinner. An epicurean when dining out, Fred directed us to a churrasco restaurant to enjoy the authentic Brazilian cuisine. Churrasco consists of beef, chicken and pork marinated in lime juice and salt, then skewered on meter-length swords and roasted over a wood fire. Beans and rice accompanied the meats. Drinks in Brazil contained a strong cane sugar liquor flavored with fresh lime juice. In the U.S., Fred enjoyed a more mundane cuisine. I think everything he ate was fried--his kitchen had a certain "greasy spoon" ambience.

Rio may be one of the world's most exciting cities, but for me gem madness was about to begin. Amazing how this quest for gemstones became an obsession. Over the years I traveled extensively in this quest, but took little time to see the country or the neighborhood in which I was doing business. I couldn't extend my buying trips to sightsee because I had too many obligations at home. So here I was in this rich, energized environment which I did not have time to thoroughly see in the first visit. Fortunately, there are weekends or at least Sundays where the buying stops for a day or two.

On our first day for gem shopping, Fred took us to see Maurice Roditi, a prominent Brazilian dealer, with a big office overlooking Copacabana Beach. Mr. Roditi produced a long black box filled with folded white papers each containing tourmalines. I carefully unfolded each paper — a dark green emerald cut, a parcel of pastel ovals, a pink cat's eye cabochon! Here I was looking at tourmalines in living color — a whole rainbow of colors — all colors! Not only was the color range spectacular, some tourmalines were bi-colors (two or more different colors in one stone). Occasionally stones contained inclusions that gave them a cat's eye. Here was one stone variety with so many different appearances. Memorable purchases of that day included a matched pair of watermelon tourmaline. They were only about two carats each, but the colors green and watermelon pink were intense and they were a perfect match. In my limited trips to the Tucson show, I hadn't seen a beautiful matched pair like these.

Tourmalines! Tourmaline is one of the birthstones for October. Before gemological knowledge and tests were developed, tourmaline wasn't known as a distinct mineral. In 1703 a parcel of mixed stones from Ceylon was sent to a cutter in Amsterdam labeled "turmali." The name tourmaline stuck and more colors were discovered. Let's establish the fact that my favorite gemstone is usually the one that I am looking at, no matter which variety it is. With tourmalines it was love at first sight. I was enamored with the stone just from looking at the pictures in the encyclopedia.

The rest of the group had spent an hour looking at stones, then departed for sightseeing with Fred. I spent the day with Mr. Roditi. Finally I wandered back to the hotel to join the group for another night of fine food and too much booze. In my sleep I dreamed of stones, mountains of them, each singing its siren song. The rest of the world was blocked out of my consciousness—I was in gemstone heaven.

The next day, Sunday, I toured with the group to visit the famous statue of Christ the Redeemer on Mt. Corcovado overlooking Rio. Here one can view the city, it's beautiful beaches and Sugarloaf Mountain. On the way to the top we passed many voodoo shrines beside the road. Candles were burning, flowers and small figurines surrounding the candles. Brazil is a truly multicultural society, populated with immigrants from around the world. Brazilians are proud of their racial tolerance. At the time of this tour Brazil was still considered a "Third World" country. Rio was a crazy wild city with high-rise buildings, great beaches, great wealth, dire poverty and boundless energy.

The third day we flew to Belo Horizonte in the state of Minas Gerais (general mining). Belo Horizonte exuded a business-like atmosphere; most of the vast mineral business in Brazil emanates from there. A gold rush drew people into the Minas Gerais area in the 1700s. The city of Ouro Preto became the early capital of Minas Gerais, when the area of Belo Horizonte was a farm. A higher altitude of around 5,000 feet creates a subtropical environment. In 1897 the capital was moved to "Cidade de Minas" and in 1906 it was renamed Belo Horizonte. At this time an early city planner, Aarao Reis, designed a city with a town center dedicated to business development. In the 1940s famous architect Oscar Niemeyer came in and created wide streets, large lakes, and parks. Immigrants from Italy, Germany, Spain, and Lebanon-Syria added a unique flavor to this city. Belo had modern amenities: paved streets, good restaurants, and decent but simple hotels. At the gem and mineral museum in Belo, I took a picture of Fred standing next to a quartz crystal point that was as tall as he was.

In Belo I had my first experience with a "suicide shower." The hotel had potable running water — cold water only. Attached to the shower head was an electrical heating device to warm the water. When it was turned on sparks flew out, crackling and hissing. Even more scary was the metal shower stall, which seemed eager for electrocution. Thus began the "cold shower" period in my life. I was ready to embrace the Third World.

A point of interest: Men in Brazil carried purses, small clutches, containing things American men would shove in their pockets. This was not a "feminine" thing, it was a macho thing. Their tight pants emphasized every muscle of the gluteus maximus. No loosy goosy trousers with pockets for these guys.

The next day we bussed to a topaz deposit on the way to Ouro Prieto. This was our "mining" day. I hadn't brought dirt digging clothes, but this was no fashion show. This deposit held topaz crystals embedded in clay. The clay was moist, so essentially we were digging through stiff mud in search of small yellow-gold topaz crystals. This is labor-intensive mining, but it is safe and easy to access. After an hour of digging in the clay-mud I caught a glimpse of a shiny crystal face. My pulse quickened as I brushed the mud off the tiny golden crystal. Ah, the thrill of the Eureka! moment.

Personally, topaz is not one of my favorite stones, but it does have an interesting history. In ancient Indian lore topaz was used to cure "dimness of vision." The topaz was to soak in wine for three days and nights. Before sleeping the patient rubbed the wine-soaked topaz over his eyes, and some wine was allowed to touch the eyeball. After that it was okay to drink the wine.

The city of Ouro Prieto was the early boom town capitol during the gold rush of the 1700s. Iron and bauxite (aluminum-bearing ore) added to the attractions in the area. It became a great cultural center featuring outstanding Baroque era architecture. Besides growing mining and industrial businesses, a mining school was developed. The wealth of the area attracted artists, mainly painters and sculptors.

We visited a church with many stone sculptures carved by a priest in the nineteenth century. They were memorable because the carvings were of saints and notable Catholics and all of them had two left feet (maybe they were right feet). Apparently the carver had one deformed foot.

Our next destination was Govenador Valadares in Minas Gerais. We bussed over yellow rolling hills that had been stripped of their hardwood trees. Valadares was much smaller than Belo Horizonte. The city was supported by the gem business. We were back to the gem orgy. I bought a parcel of aquamarines which included about twenty stones, mostly emerald cuts, each weighing between eight and fifteen carats. They were not fine quality aquamarine but pale blue and "eye clean." Saleability is a big factor in gem purchases. Of course, on a limited budget, shopping for gemstones is challenging. The gem dealer needs to know her market, what will be saleable back home, what is fashionable, what shapes and sizes will be the most marketable.

Here I found some more exotic stones, andalusite, some sodalite, and some pretty citrine. The lesser known stones hold a fascination for me. Andalusite is an exciting gemstone in theory. Its red, green, and yellow dichroism is fascinating from a scientific view point. This occurs because each axis in the crystal structure reflects out a different color. But the stone appears brownish, and brownish stones aren't the best sellers. The sodalite with its lapis lazuli color lacks the richness of lapis lazuli with its sparkly pyrite bits. It is inexpensive and somewhat pretty, but has little "wow" factor.

My philosophy was you can't sell it if you don't have it. Since the per carat prices were at the low end I took a chance with these purchases. It can be a risky and expensive business. At this time in my "career" I had no experience. I really didn't know what was out there in the gem universe. Knowing what to buy is learned the hard way: trial and error. One thing is always true: a truly beautiful gemstone, that one with the "wow factor," is always a good purchase. What is the "wow factor?" It is an intense spectacular color, a cut that intensifies the color and gives the gemstone a spectacular brilliance and is sizeable enough to attract attention! Then the questions are "Can I afford this stone? Do I have a buyer for this stone?" There are several approaches to the gem business — do the high end, shoot for the middle stuff, or sell the cheap stuff which attracts the "something for nothing" crowd. I never had the capital or the clientele for the super expensive stuff. So I went for the attractive and saleable middle range.

Beauty and price may or may not correlate. There are inexpensive stone varieties such as quartz and feldspar minerals that can have some spectacular beauty, but these may not be romantic enough or exotic enough for the retail buyer. More expensive stones of top quality may not be in the retail buyer's budget. Once my friend Valmiro Santos (whom I met in Brazil) sent me 10,000 carats of smoky quartz for the price of ten cents per carat. How much is 10,000 carats? Five carats per gram, so two kilos, or a bit over four pounds avoirdupois. The stones ranged in size from about 10 to 400 carats. What kind of quality do you get at ten cents a carat? Cheap junk! The cutting was barely acceptable, with lots of larger stones, 100 to 400 carats. I took them to a show in Santa Monica, California and sold many. That was the market for the big stones; all the stones over 100 carats sold. I asked the customers what they were going to do with the stones: put them in sculptures, use them as paper weights, or just buy them because they were big and cheap? Size can be an allure for gem material to the uninformed. I could not sell this big stuff in Reno, not because the buyers were more discriminating, but the desire for the big junk just wasn't there. Figuring out one's market takes time and experience. My attraction was always to the unusual, and that, too, sells if the stones have a bit of the "wow factor." With some more exotic stones, relaying the stone's history can spark the buyer's interest. For thousands of years gemstones have been thought to have magical qualities. Only the wealthy or powerful owned gems in the past.

The colored stone market doesn't provide a consistent flow of goods like the diamond market. It is generally dominated by smaller mining ventures in exotic places. Some years there are huge quantities of a particular gemstone. A few years later the same stone may not be available at all. Political situations may also affect the availability of some stones. Boycotts and chaos in Third World countries affect the supply. One example of market irregularities: after 9/11 it was discovered that Osama bin Laden had made some investments in tanzanite rough in Arusha, Tanzania. So tanzanite became a hot political potato and a U.S. boycott resulted. With Burma, now called Myanmar, newly mined rubies were illegal to sell in the U.S. for a few years, because the American Congress didn't like the nastiness of the political regime. A dealer could sell his old stock of Burmese rubies if purchased before the boycott. Gem dealers tend to put politics aside when it comes to business. Is that good? Think of it like this: the poor miners in gem-rich, but otherwise poor countries have mouths to feed just like the rest of us. Do you have a problem with that? The gem business actually supports a lot of poor people on the planet. Unfortunately, most remain poor.

Valadares was a great source of gems. Then it was time to board the bus for the next and final stop, Teofilo Otoni. I remember traveling through rolling hills, often rather barren, sometimes forested. Teofilo Otoni was a village, much smaller than Valadares. Gemstone rough and cutting was the primary business here. After all the dealers we had already visited, my purchases here were limited. The next day we flew back to Rio and returned home.

After recovering from jet lag and the adventure, I took my stones to the jewelers in Reno and sold quite a few. The first to go was the matched pair of watermelon tourmalines. The impossible dream was finally realized — I was a gem dealer!

- Lesson seven: My best purchases were the affordable stones with some "wow."

## Chapter 4 - First Gem Shows

Fall, 1978

Now I had some gem inventory and I was ready to find a wider market. A gem show came to Reno and I had a one-table space. The public liked my stones and bought a few gems. The producer of this show had exhibitor space in Tucson for the February show, so I signed up for a good space in the Marriott Hotel on the mezzanine on "gemstone row." By now I had some gem dealer acquaintances and could find new sources of gems. It's strange how serendipitous events took me to my new "fantasy" job.

February, 1979--Tucson

A small mineral show had begun in 1955 in Tucson, Arizona. Arizona is a rock hound's dream with fabulous copper minerals, like azurite and chrysocolla, mined at Bisbee and Morenci. Numerous turquoise deposits dot the state. Peridot and amethyst are also commercially mined there. What started out a small show held at a grammar school developed into the biggest gem and mineral show in the world. Tucson was a fairly quiet city in 1977 when I first visited it. It had a distinctive western feeling, with dude ranches and plenty of cowboy musical groups. The elegant setting of the city gives the feeling of wide open spaces surrounded by the Sonoran Desert and mountains that can be snow tipped in February. Usually the temperature hovers around 70 degrees in the winter, luring dealers from cold places around the world. Even back in the '70s there were excellent four star restaurants. Now the show has grown over the years and has over forty venues in hotels, motels, tent-covered parking lots, and various multi-use buildings. Vendors come from all over the world selling the obvious gems and minerals, pashmina scarves, singing bowls and other exotic imports. The cowboy music groups seem to have disappeared. .

Tucson was comparatively simple then. It was a big mineral exposition attended by some western and international gem dealers. Steve accompanied me to the show which was open 10 a.m. to 9 p.m. Booth space cost $600 and came with a 6-foot table. The eleven-hour show day prohibited us from going out to dinner and seemed endless. Truthfully, no one buys gemstones after 6 p.m. After the first evening of sitting around talking to other bored-to-death dealers for three nonproductive hours, the next evening we brought in a case of champagne, a bucket of ice, and plastic cups. Time not particularly well spent, but it was fun. The first year wasn't very profitable, but this was an opportunity to get acquainted with the other eccentrics. One must be rather eccentric or just plain crazy to be in the gem business. The job kept us from enjoying a week in Tucson with perfect weather.

Summer, 1979

One day a nicely dressed middle-aged man came into my office in Reno for a jewelry appraisal. At the time I didn't know this would be another life-changing moment. He handed me a beautifully carved wood box containing a selection of very fine men's rings. Fine star sapphires, chrysoberyl cat's eye, and fancy colored sapphire cabochons were set into expertly crafted 18K gold mountings. As a gemologist it was exciting to see such exceptional work and fine gemstones. Most of my work consisted of appraising diamond rings, earrings, and pendants. Larger diamonds needed a diagram mapping the inclusions. These diagrams helped to determine the clarity grade of the diamond and could be used to identify the stone, like a fingerprint. I couldn't finish appraising all these pieces in the first appointment so he returned the next day.

Lenard Taylor lived in Bangkok and worked for Aramco, recruiting Thais to work in the Saudi Arabian oil fields. Every year he came to Reno to visit his brother. He explained that originally he worked in Vietnam for Aramco and had escaped on the last boat out of Saigon during the Vietnamese War. He was then transferred to the Philippines and finally to Bangkok. All these Asian locations had fine stones and master jewelers. He had a great gem dealer in Bangkok and if I wanted to come over he would introduce me to the dealer. This was an opportunity I was not going to pass up. Again, out of the blue I had a meeting that would take me on a new adventure.

October 6, 1979--Bangkok, Thailand

One of my friends, Liz Summers, learned of my trip to Bangkok and wanted to join me. After twenty-four hours of travel we landed in steamy hot Bangkok. Before the 21st century airport security regulations, the journey to Bangkok from Reno lasted a minimum of 24 hours. If you didn't book your trip carefully it might take longer. And this was before you had to show up two hours in advance. If I was flying to the Orient, traveling from Reno meant flying to San Francisco, Los Angeles or Seattle to catch an international flight. West Coast flights didn't fly nonstop to Bangkok, so I'd have to change planes in Tokyo, Hong Kong, or Taipei. Before flights I began to collect books that could take my mind off the long boring hours spent in flight and in airports.

Lenard met us at the airport and we were his guests at a traditional Thai-style home off Sukumvit Road, on Soi 49. The home was two storied with mahogany trim and ample windows. The interior was beautifully decorated with mango and watermelon colored Thai silk upholstery. Highly polished dark teak wood floors and doors contrasted with white walls. I heard a rumor that there was hot water in the showers, but I never found it. More cold showers! But when the temperature is 90 degrees a cold shower is very pleasant. Fresh flowers, often sprays of small orchids, in all the rooms added to the elegance. Len's maid, Sunni, cooked the meals and cleaned the house. Previously she had worked for a French doctor and cooked western style food unless you requested Thai food.

My memories three decades later are all about the fabulous meals. Seafood! My favorite restaurant was on Sukumvit Road. It was a large open area with three walls covered by a metal roof. At the back end was a long portion set up like the meat section of a supermarket filled with ice and all sorts of seafood: giant Burmese prawns, smaller prawns, lobsters, and endless varieties of whole fish. You were met by a waitress with a shopping cart. You'd choose your fish, then go to the produce section on the other side and choose your very fresh vegetables. Everything was fresh picked or caught that day. In the front the chefs awaited your cooking instructions for all the different Thai specialties. At Len's house Sunni prepared excellent food; one morning I was served a platter with twelve different kinds of fruit. I could name six of the fruits, the other six still remain unidentified. Very strong dark roast coffee accompanied fresh baked banana bread and eggs. First class!

The tiny streets off Sukumvit Road were laid out in an illogical maze pattern. I would awaken at the first signs of dawn, go out and walk around viewing life in Thailand. Bangkok is noisy; an ambient noise level of a busy city seemed constant, except about 5 a.m. Dawn seemed to be a special quiet time. Somewhere in this maze of streets was a mosque. When it was especially quiet I could hear the 5:45 prayer being broadcast through a loud speaker to the faithful. I searched for the mosque, listening for the sound of the prayer as a beacon. Carefully I memorized the directions to the mosque to avoid getting lost. On these early morning forays I would see the Buddhist monks with their rice bowls seeking their morning meal. These special walks showed me the beauty and harmony of the simple Thai life. By 6:30 in the morning all the beauty seemed to disappear, the extraordinary busy-ness resumed and the darker sides of Thai life became more visible.

My first trip to Thailand was all about gems. The first day we taxied to New Road to meet Mr. Apichart, owner of a small jewelry store and gem dealer. This tourist area was lined with silk shops, souvenir stands, jewelry stores and dimly lit houses of prostitution. One could peek in the windows of the brothels and see very young women waiting for their customers. On the sidewalks spicy Thai food cooked on small braziers exuded mouth-watering aromas into the streets.

On this first visit to Thailand, men wore sarongs, very sexy. By my next visit the sarongs were being replaced by jeans. Globalization crept like a plague destroying the cultures and traditions of the Asian world. Thailand was rapidly changing. Bangkok streets were crowded with exhaust-spewing taxis and tuktuks. One day Liz and I left New Road in a tuktuk, an open three-wheeled motorized vehicle. It was a great way to breathe in carbon monoxide and I ended up with a few hours of carbon monoxide poisoning. I felt nauseated and sleepy. After a quick nap at Lenard's house I felt revived.

New Road parallels the Chao Phraya River carrying boats filled with all kinds of merchandise. A large Buddhist complex faces the river in one part of town. Golden spires top the temples, giving an other-worldly heavenly appearance. Canals thread through the city. Larger canals created watery neighborhoods where you could do all your shopping from canoe-like boats.

The Oriental Hotel, just off New Road, had patio dining adjacent to the river. Len took us there for lunch to enjoy Tom Yam Goong (hot and sour shrimp soup) accompanied by Singha beer. We sat by the river filled with endless boat traffic watching the world go by, profusely sweating under the 90 degree Thai sun. This was the ultimate business lunch.

Besides living large, there was work. Yes, gem buying is work. Apichart was a slender young Thai, very smart and ready to help us find good gem buys. In Apichart's shop we spent a couple of days looking at parcels of gems — rubies, sapphires, zircons, and spinels. I found the natural colored zircons interesting; they have earthy colors — yellows, oranges, and browns and rare reds. They have a high refractive index giving them exceptional brilliance. Spinels come in a rainbow of colors and have a fairly high refractive index. Most exciting spinels are hot pink and hot red colors. These hot colors don't resemble rubies — they are much brighter. Some of the red spinels do resemble rubies and in ancient times they were referred to as balas rubies. Apichart also had some "fancy sapphires," those with colors of pink, yellow, green, orange, and violet. These are generally less expensive than the fine blue ones. I think the violet shades are particularly beautiful and at this time they had bargain prices. Fine oranges and intense pink sapphires have always had premium prices.

On Saturday, we were booked to visit the ruby market in Chantaburi. East of Bangkok, bordering Cambodia, are numerous alluvial deposits of rubies and sapphires. Individual miners buy small sections in the river gravels to pan out the rich corundum deposits. Monsoon rains fall from summer to mid-October providing river flow that washes up new gravels. Rubies and sapphires are the primary gemstones mined in Thailand, but there are exotic stones, such as zircons and spinels, also found in the gravels. Imports from Burma and Sri Lanka add to the gemstone selection in Thailand.

Before dawn, we boarded a bus with bone-chilling air conditioning and headed east to Chantaburi. This was my first time out to buy expensive gems and I was advised that these would be tough buying conditions. It was important that I had to apply my book knowledge to the real world. Poor choices could be costly. There are many factors to consider. Color is the critical determinant in valuing rubies and sapphires. Inclusions (internal crystals, cracks, and minerals) affect the price. The origins of rubies and sapphires also influence the price. Thai rubies and sapphires are not the most prized, lacking the intensity of the Burmese rubies. Sapphires from Sri Lanka have more intense blue colors. The quality of the cut of the stone will determine its brilliance and beauty, thus the price. Size is always a factor in the ultimate value of the stone. At this time stones from Burma and Sri Lanka often had "native cuts" – proportions and polish were poor. These stones didn't have the quality finish demanded by western standards. Thai cutting was acceptable, so these "native cuts" were recut in Thailand to appeal to a more discerning market.

On arrival we were guided to a table on the sidewalk under an overhanging roof. We were seated across from a dealer. This was a no frills operation. Runners brought in specially folded papers containing rubies and sapphires. There were no instruments available for a thorough examination of a stone to determine the quality or if it might be a synthetic. I was armed with a tiny penlight. It was like going into battle with a paper sword. So with only a mighty penlight, I placed each stone table (the top facet) down over the light. Almost magically I could see the microscopic inclusions and any color zoning in the gem to determine if it was a natural stone, not a synthetic.

Thai rubies were readily available, but they are generally a darker red. Burmese rubies are considered the best rubies, but at this time Burma rubies were not readily available because of restrictions from the Burmese government. Burmese ruby availability is mostly a matter of political policy — too often bad political policy.

Thai blue sapphires tend to be a dark blue with little intensity. Blue sapphires with a more desirable color are mined in Sri Lanka. Rumor has it that sapphires from Kashmir are the best, but looking for one is like going on a snipe hunt. The mine in Kashmir is located in the northwest portion of the Himalayas at an elevation of nearly 15,000 feet which is snow covered most of the year. Green sapphires are abundant in Thailand, but their "army green" color holds little appeal in the gem market.

Most of the gems were natural stones, but occasionally a synthetic stone might be passed around. It's a risky business so you need to know what you are doing. I managed to buy a couple of stones that were very saleable.

If you wanted a parcel, you would tape the paper shut, sign your name, and write your offer. Bargaining was required! Lighting conditions were less than perfect. Monsoon rain fell intermittently, creating more darkness. After about three hours of this rather tense work, carts with grilled skewered chicken sate rolled through the streets.

The sate was served in paper with plastic bags of peanut sauce. A perfect ending to an exciting day.

We returned to Bangkok Saturday night. On Sunday the gem business shuts down. Len, Liz, and I hailed a taxi to the immense Sunday Market. This market was supported by the locals, it wasn't just for the tourists. I think you could buy almost anything there. There were stalls with dogs and other domestic pets, snakes, anything of a household nature, food, ceramics, fabrics, things legal and perhaps some illegal. We wandered around most of the day. I bought some blue and white ceramics, brass knuckles, a sarong, and a silk scarf. Why did I buy the brass knuckles? In the back of my mind I thought they could be a defense for myself if I ever needed them.

Patpong Street represents the more prurient side of Bangkok. It is located about a mile from New Road. Night clubs with all sorts of stuff: women removing razor blades from their crotches and maybe more disgusting things going on. I don't think I'm a prude, I just don't want to see women degrade themselves — this offends my feminist side. One Sunday morning Apichart brought us to brunch on Patpong Street. (There were no shows in the mornings.) This fabulous seafood restaurant had a tank swimming with shrimp. The chef reached into the tank with a strainer, filled it with shrimp, then marched to a kettle of boiling water, cooked the shrimp for a couple of minutes, dumped them on a platter and served them plain without any sauce. Very fresh.

Maybe this trip to Thailand sounds like it was all partying and shopping, but in reality we worked six days a week and crowded in the fun stuff on Sundays and evenings. Stone choices were critical to the success of my business — it's all speculation and choices eventually become intuitive. I quickly forgot all those beautiful tourmalines from Brazil and had fallen for the more exotic sapphires and spinels. Okay, I am fickle! Returning home, without the maid and tropical fruits and the aura of excitement of Bangkok, was a return to reality that I needed.

- Lesson Eight: Avoid tuktuks, too much carbon monoxide.

## Chapter 5 - THE DEEPDENE MYSTERY

January 1980 Reno, Nevada

Dr. Pough's life experiences were constantly being revealed, facet by facet. Fred had received an invitation, expenses paid, to go to Idar-Oberstein, Germany to resolve the question of whether the 104 carat Deepdene diamond had been irradiated to give it the strong yellow color of a "fancy colored diamond."The Deepdene is a stone with a "name;" it is included in the books on famous diamonds. Any gemstone with a "name" is extremely important. This could be the most exciting meeting ever! Wow! Could a neophyte in the gem business like me miss this important meeting? "Can I go?" I asked Fred when I heard he was going on this mission.

This infamous Deepdene was shrouded in mystery. It was mined in South Africa in the 1890s. In 1954 the jeweler Harry Winston bought the diamond from a Mr. and Mrs. Bok of Philadelphia. Winston sold the diamond to a Canadian buyer in 1955. The Deepdene appeared again in 1971 at a Christie's auction in Geneva. Before the auction the Deepdene was examined by the German Gemmological (European spelling) Laboratory and the University of Mainz; both institutions concluded the Deepdene had a natural yellow color. Apparently some experts decided that the diamond was too large to be irradiated. Swiss gemologist Dr. Edward Gubelin examined the diamond at the auction; he stated that the stone had been irradiated. In spite of Gubelin's opinion the diamond was purchased by Van Cleef and Arpels. Next the diamond was retested in London by the Gem Testing Laboratory. The gem lab substantiated Gubelin's irradiation claim, so Van Cleef and Arpels, the French jewelry company, returned the questionable Deepdene to Christie's. The reputation of the Deepdene Diamond as an "important" stone was sullied. The trail of the diamond grows cold here.

This Deepdene, irradiated or not, was worth several million dollars. But how many million depended on its treatment. Before irradiation the Deepene was undoubtedly an insipid pale yellow. Irradiation would make the stone more attractive. There are several factors determining the value of diamonds and other gemstones. Irradiation of diamonds began in the early 1900s when a pale yellow diamond (referred to as a "cape" diamond) was exposed to radium for a few days. The diamond turned green and retained the radiation, leaving a "hot" (radioactive) stone. Later diamonds were irradiated in a cyclotron resulting in a color change. These, too, emitted radiation. When they were heated the color stabilized and radioactivity disappeared.

Other factors affecting value are summed up as the "Four C's". **Carat weight** is determined by weighing a stone on a specially calibrated gem scale. One carat is the equivalent of .20 gram. Generally the larger a gemstone will sell more per carat weight. Exceptions would be stones that naturally form into large crystals or masses such as quartz gems, feldspars, and lapis lazuli.

**Clarity** is determined when diamonds are graded under a microscope using 10 power magnification. The internal occupants, crystals and cracks, of a stone are called "inclusions." Crystals and fractures are commonly found inside of gemstones. Even very minute inclusions affect the value of a diamond.

All gemstones are valued on **color**. Generally stones with the most intense colors are the most valuable. Diamonds are found in many colors in nature. "Fancy colors"--pinks, greens, blues, reds, and intense yellows--are rare and demand premium prices. Brown and black diamonds are somewhat common and sell for lower prices than the "colorless diamonds." Colorless diamonds, most commonly found in jewelry, actually range from truly colorless to very pale yellows. These very pale yellows "face up" as colorless. Truly colorless diamonds are the more valuable with the prices decreasing as they approach a visible pale yellow or are slightly brown. These off-colored diamonds can be irradiated to become a "fancy color."

**Cut** determines the ultimate beauty of a gemstone Faceting must be precise and symmetrical. Proportions of depth to width are critical factors creating the "brilliance" of the gem. Polish creates the ultimate luster of the gem.

Origin may be a big factor in valuing some stones ( i.e., "Colombian emerald," "Burmese ruby"). Diamond values are not affected by the origin of the stone.

In 1980 Herr Frederich, a jeweler from Frankfurt, Germany showed up in possession of the Deepdene. He wanted to sell the diamond and needed to find out the diamond's genealogy since the stone had a questionable provenance. He contacted Fred to resolve this matter.

Fred flew to Germany a week before the big event. He told me to fly to Frankfurt and catch the train in the station underneath the airport. Piece of cake! Right?

February 22, 1980--Frankfurt, Germany

The Frankfurt Airport is a small city with shopping -a person could live in the airport. Expensive designer shops proliferate in the entry to the departure lounges of the airport. The more obscure layers of the airport house grocery stores, movie theaters, porn shops, and an important train station.

Since this wasn't my first international trip, I felt very confident that taking the train to Idar-Oberstein was simple. I proceeded to take escalators down to the bowels of the airport, bought a ticket to Idar-Oberstein and was told to go to Track 4 and board the next incoming train. I boarded the train and bought a cup of steaming rich European coffee and sat down feeling very content. About twenty minutes later, a woman came up to me and told me to get off at the next station, then to go to Track 3 and catch the next train coming through there. I didn't realize that the first train I boarded was the express to Paris. How weird! Who was this woman and how did she know where I was going? Nevertheless I followed her instructions after confirming it was truly the Paris express. I found a comfortable seat on the second train, got another cup of coffee and enjoyed looking at the German countryside. About forty minutes later another woman came up to me and told me to get off at the next stop and proceed to Track 2. What was going on? Again I followed this stranger's instructions. After a short ride I arrived at Idar-Oberstein. To this day I am clueless who these women were, but very thankful for the mysterious guidance. Was there some mystic force at work?

When I caught up to Fred I told him of my train experience. "Oh, I forgot to tell you to 'umslagen'." So I went back to the train station and read the signs. There is a list showing where the train stops when you need to change trains. "Umslagen" apparently means change. Whoever those guardian angels were, they might not be on my next adventure.

Idar-Oberstein consists of two villages that grew into each other. Both were located in a rocky canyon along the Nahr River. Buildings tended to be two-or three-story stone structures neatly arranged side by side. This part of Germany is in the Schwarzwald (Black Forest) area. There are tracts of forest with small conifers growing so close together that it is almost dark in the interior (if you are nutty enough to try walk through them).

Finally I had arrived at the destination with a reputation of having the finest colored gemstones. The surrounding countryside contains chalcedony, jasper and quartz deposits. In the 1400s Idar and Oberstein became centers for gem carving and cutting. Water-driven grinding wheels were used to cut the local materials into functional vessels, cameos, and gems. With an abundance of banded chalcedonies (agates) they created vessels with striped patterns. They dyed agates to intensify the banding. Dyeing of agates dates back to Roman times. Agates are not naturally black; somehow the Romans found that banded agates could be boiled in a sugar solution, then treated with sulfuric acid to give some bands a black color. Ancient cameos are proof of this technology –one wonders who was fooling around by boiling stones in sugar water. An orange-red color results from boiling the stones in various iron compounds. The Germans developed blue, green, and yellow dye formulas.

In the 1800s the Germans went to Brazil and brought back rough gem materials and developed a cutting center where gem rough was cut and polished into some of the world's finest gemstones. Some German dealers decided that the delicious Brazilian churrasco could be adapted back home. The Germans created "speissbraten" which is pork marinated in onion juice and salt, then roasted in an open wood fire. It's served with French fries and a marinated vegetable salad. In retrospect, I wonder if the cuisine in all these places is more exciting than the gemstones, especially the French fries!

Personally I loved the German gems, but successful buying in Germany depended on the money markets. If the dollar was high in value, I could buy German stones and still be competitive on the American market. A strong

Deutsche mark made the stones too expensive, when looking at the price in dollars.

The meeting day arrived. Ten men, cutters and diamond experts, gathered in front of the building, and Fred and I joined them. We introduced ourselves, all speaking in English. Soon a dark green Rolls Royce drove up to the meeting place. The chauffeur got out of the car, opened the back door and a middle aged man stepped out. Herr Frederich was extremely gracious and took my hand and kissed it. (Where have I been all my life? This doesn't happen in Reno.) I was the only woman in attendance and the only non-German speaking person there. What a privilege for me. We went into the hall and sat down in straight-backed chairs in a circle. Once the proceedings began, the language was all in German. Dr. Gubelin was not in attendance, but he phoned in from Switzerland. Frederich pulled a blue velvet box out of his coat pocket. The box was opened and there was the brilliant cushion-shaped yellow Deepdene. Frederich removed the stone and passed it around. As the gem came to me, my hands shook a bit while I held it and examined it. It was about the size of a small lime with a deep yellow hue. The culet (the smallest facet on the bottom of the stone, which prevents chipping on the lower point) was a bit large. I turned the diamond around to catch the reflections of the facets. The stone's dispersion produced magical rainbows. Its golden brilliance flashed like a loud sound in the silent room. I was dumbstruck. Reluctantly I passed the stone to the next person. Then Fred produced a small white container with a space that held the Deepdene perfectly. This was the container in which Fred had irradiated the stone in the 1950s for Harry Winston. Frederich wanted to know if the stone could be recut to remove the effects of irradiation. Apparently in a diamond this size, irradiation is close to the surface, so recutting could take it back to the original color, in theory. This idea had not been widely tested. The local cutters did not want to risk recutting on this unusual diamond. Of course I did not understand one word of the conversation until Fred explained it to me later. The meeting ended and we all went to the restaurant at the Schwann Hotel. Lunch was wonderful and conversation reverted to English as we enjoyed the cream of peppercorn soup. (Best soup I ever had—at least in Europe! )

What has happened to the Deepdene? Maybe it is languishing in its golden brilliance in that blue velvet box on a shelf in some jeweler's safe. Or perhaps it is hanging around someone's neck in the Middle East. As far as I know the stone retains its underground existence.

The next day Fred took me to a dinner meeting with some of his gem cronies. Again, I was the only woman that had ever attended one of the meetings—another honor! English language prevailed during the meeting. The man I sat next to spoke unaccented English and I commented on how good his English was. He laughed and said, "I was a prisoner of war and held in Virginia."

Feeling very sympathetic, I said, "I'm sorry."

"No, no," he responded. "I was well fed and well cared for. I was one of the lucky ones." At the end of WWII, Germans were out of food and people starved.

Fred took me around to some of the gem cutters the next day. I met one cutter who specialized in small calibrated gemstones. These stones are cut to standard sizes so they fit into standard sized mountings. I found some beautiful tourmalines at another cutter. This opened up another source of gems, if I could buy them at competitive prices. Working with the Germans is great. They are efficient and very professional dealers. They take pride in their work and deserve a premium price. Now I had another source for exquisite gem stones, greater possibilities as long as the dollar was strong.

There was one more big event that week. The Olympics in Lake Placid were televised in Germany. We watched the U.S.A. hockey team beat the U.S.S.R. team!

- Lesson Nine: When you arrive in a new place, ask a lot of questions when traveling by train, bus, or boat. Assume nothing.

## Chapter 6 - BEYOND BANGKOK–BURMA

September 26, 1980--Bangkok

On my return to Bangkok I was accompanied with a small entourage. This was Fred Pough's first trip to the Orient. My friend, Betty Anne Mahoney, a registered nurse who had served in Vietnam during the Tet Offensive, had never been to Thailand. She came into my office one day expressing an interest in gems and we began a friendship. Together we descended on Lenard's hospitality. After recovering from the long flight, Betty Anne and I had our couture moment at the silk shop owned by Apichart's wife. Her shop was next to his jewelry store on New Road. Brilliant colored Thai silks arranged in bolts by color in solids, stripes and plaids lined the walls. First, the clerks took our measurements, then we would work with Mrs. Apichart on design and finding the perfect fabric. Beautiful, well-made clothing would be finished before we left Bangkok. Our priorities were obvious.

The next day Apichart had planned a trip to the ruby market in Chantaburi. BettyAnne's next stop was the pharmacy to buy Larium (that poisonous malaria medicine that has been found to create psychosis if taken too long). BettyAnne had checked with the Centers for Disease Control and Prevention in Atlanta, and they recommended we take this poison to prevent getting malaria when we went to Burma, our next destination after Chantaburi. BettyAnne insisted we take this precaution, even though the medicine could not be purchased legally in the U.S.A. (That should have been a clue.)

Bright sunshine gave us good light in the Chantaburi ruby market. We spent the morning opening gem papers examining rubies and sapphires. For Fred and BettyAnne the ruby market was like a sit down Oriental market. Each parcel contained a new surprise, but this was to be short lived. Abruptly at noon Apichart announced we were going on a boat trip. After a short drive we arrived at a dock on the Bay of Siam and boarded a rickety old fishing boat. Brilliant blue skies, smooth turquoise to sapphire blue seas promised a marvelous day. BettyAnne began a search for life jackets the minute we boarded the old tub. No life jackets! BettyAnne was not enjoying this adventure. An ebullient Fred seated himself on the prow as we sailed to deeper waters. Way out in the bay the boat engines stopped and we were each given an oil can with a string line and hook and live bait so we could fish for our lunch. Fred was having a good old time; BettyAnne sulked. I lowered my line and a few minutes later pulled up a small octopus. Dumb luck! This was considered a delicacy and everybody was excited over my catch. It didn't take long before we had enough seafood to grill for lunch. Our fresh catch cooked on open charcoal braziers was served with rice. I was thinking this was a fabulous day when suddenly rain clouds formed and blustery winds stirred up the sea. As soon as the monsoon rains started to pelt down, BettyAnne headed for the pilot house with an incredible look of fear on her face. Fred and I headed for the prow where wind and rain created a fine spray on our faces as the boat turned towards land. The storm had passed by the time we docked. The blue skies returned and the sea took on its jewel tones once again.

A few weeks later back in Reno, Steve and I were having dinner with BettyAnne and her husband Jerry. I expounded on the great adventure on the Bay of Siam, going on about how beautiful a day it was. BettyAnne whined about the treacherous boat trip that had endangered our lives in a terrible storm at sea. Steve and

Jerry looked at each other and asked if we had been on the same trip. Perception is reality and we all live in our own realities.

Back in Bangkok, Len, Fred, BettyAnne and I had spent the day on New Road looking through gemstone parcels of dark red Thai rubies. Rubies are placed in gem papers with yellow liner papers; this makes the color appear better. Lenard had quit his job with Aramco and partnered with Apichart. About five o'clock we caught a taxi for Len's house. The full moon created floods during the monsoon season. As we turned onto Sukumvit, the rains hit in full fury, and the flood waters got deeper and deeper. Soon the water was higher than the bottom of the taxi's door and water started to flow inthrough rust holes in the floor. The big question arose: if the water was higher than the bottom of the door, could we still open the door? We felt a bit desperate. Finally the taxi pulled over to higher ground and we piled out into the knee-deep water. We landed near a store that had Wellington style boots and plastic flip flops. Fred opted for the Wellies; Len, BettyAnne and I went for the flip flops. In the muddy deep water we couldn't see where were stepping. That was a bit scary--the sewers ran in shallow channels covered by rectangular concrete blocks paralleling the streets. Sometimes these blocks were removed, leaving the sewer exposed. Were we walking through sewage or would we fall into one of the holes to the sewer? Progress went very slowly. Finally we slogged down our street, Soi 49, and as we traveled through the maze to Len's house we gained a bit of altitude so the water was only a few inches deep. As we approached Len's house we began to laugh about this perilous little journey. The rest of the evening we laughed and drank (way too much). I woke up with a headache and packed for the trip to Burma.

October 1, 1980 — Rangoon, Burma

We entered Burma leaving free society back in another world. Burmese immigration required us to declare all our cash and credit cards. After that ordeal we taxied past the ghost town-looking buildings to the Strand Hotel. The streets were relatively quiet compared to the extreme busyness in Bangkok. It looked like time stopped in 1942 when Japan invaded Burma. Water worn wooden buildings had long lost their original paint. Skies were gray and overcast, the people seemed to reflect the grayness of the skies.

Burma suffered under a repressive military government. The British had invaded Burma in the early 1800s and made it part of the British Empire. After the end of World War II, the Japanese left Burma and the British resumed control. In 1948 Burma was granted independence from Great Britain. A parliamentary government was installed and ruled until 1962. Then a military regime took control and put a stranglehold on the Burmese people. Markets were totally under control of the government.

The Strand Hotel was one of the most elegant hotels in Asia in the 1920s when the partying British were in charge. The hotel looked like it had stood still in time. Everything appeared to be the original that was built in 1920. As we entered the decrepit lobby, a small man in a gray Mao suit was sweeping sand off the floor. Suspicious eyes followed us to the check-in desk. Were our conversations going to be monitored? Were there bugs in our rooms other than the six legged kind? Betty Anne and I shared a room containing a 1920 claw foot bathtub. There was a hot water faucet and a cold water faucet. There would be no warm water coming out of the faucet—how would I wash my hair? At least in the tub the two temperature extremes could be mixed for warm water—so how could I complain? It wouldn't be another cold shower.

Burma has some of the richest gem deposits in the world. The state politics didn't allow free market exploitation. Free market mining and distribution could bring many Burmese out of their state of poverty, but buying and selling by private parties was not approved by the government. The government does have an "official" gem auction by invitation only. Countries with these policies end up with underground markets. Nobody ends up profiting in this atmosphere of fear and repression. So we were here only to view. If we found a parcel we wanted, it would magically show up in Bangkok a month or so later. Burma and Thailand share a long porous border. The Thais would invoice the goods thus legitimizing them for export. As a gem importer it was my obligation to declare any purchase coming into the U.S.A. and I would arrange to have a customs broker do the paperwork. The broker would meet me in the U.S. Customs section at the airport and legitimize the imports. Most gemstones are duty free, but declaring them and filling out the necessary paperwork is obligatory.

Lenard had arranged a contact to take us to see the available gem supply. We visited old homes that once housed the British colonists. One home had been quite elegant in its day; it still had a baby grand piano in the main room, but it appeared that the house hadn't been painted since 1939. When we left this house our guide whispered, "That was the minister of trade's home."Feelings of fear and insecurity welled up. Were we being watched? Would we be able to leave Burma? But Len had been here before and knew how to conduct business.

The choice of gems was limited. Surprisingly we did not see fine rubies or sapphires or any of the more exotic stones like zircon or peridot. Had there been rubies and sapphires, they may not have been affordable. But there were a few items of great rarity. I found a parcel of red and pink spinel crystals – small cubes of brilliant red and hot pinks. Spinel was unusual on the gem market at this time. A lack of familiarity made these stones a speculative buy. Beauty and rarity are saleable. The time for spinel to come to the American market was due. Its history needed to be explored. My favorite selling point became, "The most famous 'ruby' in the world, the Prince Edward ruby, is a 170 carat spinel set right in the center of the British Imperial State Crown." It's the big amorphous, lumpy, bright red stone set just above the 317 carat Cullinan 2 diamond. Like other gemstones with names, the Prince Edward ruby (spinel) has a shady if not criminal past. Edward of Woodstock, also called the "Black Prince," acquired the title when his tomb was opened in Canterbury Cathedral in the 1500s. He had been buried in black armor. Edward was given the fabulous spinel by Pedro the Cruel of Spain after killing Abu Said, the ruler of Granada. Edward proudly wore the spinel in his breast plate as he returned home. The stone had acquired the reputation of being a powerful talisman. Later in the battle of Agincourt, 1415, King Henry V wore the stone in his helmet while defeating the French.

I picked out a parcel of small faceted red spinels that desperately needed recutting. Betty Anne found a necklace made with high carat gold and fine "imperial" jadeite. "Imperial jade" has a brilliant green color, resembling that of an emerald. The stones were small, but the color and transparency were spectacular. This was a real find and where else would something like this appear? I saw a small parcel of star sapphires with a variety of "fancy colors" that I couldn't resist. In the three days we were there, some of the same parcels we had already seen showed up in subsequent viewings. The parcels we wanted were sealed, the buyer's name was written on the paper. We were assured the goods would eventually get to Bangkok. We had to have faith in this system. Our success depended on factors unknown to us. Only time would tell.

BettyAnne and I shopped for souvenirs. If tourists wanted to buy trinkets or souvenirs, they had to be purchased at government-owned shops. If not, the items could not be taken out of the country. Search and seizure was common at the airport. BettyAnne had not declared her credit cards when we went through customs (I don't know why, maybe she didn't understand the need to do this). When she tried to use her credit cards at the state stores, she was denied their use. She was upset at this, but there really wasn't much to buy.

After the disappointing shopping trip, we had a delicious Burmese-style dinner at a little hole-in-the wall restaurant Len had found. After dinner we all met in BettyAnne's and my room. Earlier in the day Betty Anne had insisted I take the Larium pill. This was really silly because we didn't see any mosquitoes in Rangoon. Maybe, to her, this was a "better safe than sorry" attitude. And at that time Larium's hideous side effects weren't disclosed. That evening I experienced horrible stomach pains, approaching those of childbirth. I spent the night rolled up in a tight ball, while the others sipped brandy and discussed religion and politics. When the evening began there were two liter bottles, one of brandy and one whiskey, that Len had carried in from Bangkok. I was totally out of it and unaware of the evening's events. When I awoke in the morning, the pains were gone and the two liter bottles were empty. Around 8 a.m. Len, BettyAnne and I had breakfast in the hotel. Fred did not show up. Finally I went up to his room and knocked on the door, and knocked and knocked. No answer. Several minutes passed and I was still knocking. Finally the door opened. Fred appeared with a bruise on his forehead, but he was totally coherent. We had a busy day of running around and Fred uttered no complaints. He never complained and led an active life well into his nineties. I wonder if the alcohol acted as a preservative for him.

Rangoon has one spectacular tourist site: a vast Buddhist temple complex. Golden Burmese-style domes and Thai-style domes intermix in this huge site, as they do in Bangkok's large temple site. Burma and Thailand have a long history of conflict. One country would overrun the other, leaving architectural legacy in the form of Buddhist temples.

We had to remove our shoes to enter these temples. Each temple had individual art styles reflecting the period in which it was built. Buddha was usually sitting in lotus position with a serene smile on his face. These Buddhas are usually represented with healthy slender bodies rather than the chubby ones seen in Chinese art, or the more emaciated Buddhas seen in India. Beautiful tile work floors and walkways lined the complex throughout. Unfortunately I developed athlete's foot during this barefoot tour. At least, that can be cured easily.

Poverty was the rule in Burma, with rundown buildings and sad-looking people. The contrast between Burma and Thailand is shocking. Burma and Thailand both have the same ethnic peoples who mostly share Buddhism as their religious beliefs. Geography, weather, and natural resources are similar. The big difference is the political and economic structure. Thailand has a democratic monarchy. Burma, now Myanmar, has a repressive military dictatorship. Although there is poverty in Thailand, there is a growing middle class. Jobs are available in a growing manufacturing economy. The Thais seemed happy and friendly in 1980. The prevailing repression and depression of the Burmese was obvious.

- Lesson ten: When entering a new country, find out the rules and regulations concerning money, credit cards, etc.

## Chapter 7 - CERTS: GEM MARKET GOES CRAZY

February, 1981--Tucson

Early in 1981 the U.S. was experiencing "stagflation." Interest rates were in the double digits and investors were looking for new markets to invest their money. Gold and silver prices shot up. Suddenly gemstones appeared as an investment possibility. Diamonds, rubies, and sapphires were sent to gem laboratories for certification to supposedly give gemstones credence as an investment for potential investors. Certification entails examination by a gemological laboratory and assigning a "grade" to the stone's color, cut, and clarity. Sometimes origin of the stone would be stated. Buying a certified stone was more about buying a piece of paper with a gemologist's grading system than looking at the stone and assessing the gem's visible beauty. Where money flows, energy goes. Now the Tucson show was hit by dozens of barely post-pubescent Gordon Gecko types from Fairfield, Iowa, hyping certificated gemstones as an investment opportunity. These hustlers didn't look at stones, unaware of any "wow" factor, they were essentially selling "certs." No one seemed concerned about a secondary market to resell the "hard asset investments." Apparently nobody saw that this was a "bubble" market that would eventually burst into obscurity. Thai rubies were readily available and prices were escalating. I had the source for rubies — Apichart and Lenard were at the source. They would buy the stones, send them to me, I would get them certified. Cool deal? Maybe?

BettyAnne and I drove the 1,000 miles from Reno to the gem show in Tucson that year. The road from Reno to Las Vegas goes through some of the most desolate land in the country. Brothels are the points of interest between Tonopah and Vegas. After gassing up the car in Kingman, Arizona, we headed south into the verdant Sonoran desert with mesquite, saguaros, palo verde trees, and beaver tail cactus. The next day we met the plane from Los Angeles to pick up Lenard. This flight was full of dealers from L.A. carrying suitcases full of gems. How much gem wealth must have been on that flight? Millions and millions. A couple of years later gems would be shipped to the show from all over the country by Brinks rather than hand carried.

A few days later Steve and Sydney flew in for the end of the show. One night Len, BettyAnne, Steve, Sydney and I had a late dinner at my favorite Arizona style Mexican restaurant. I was the designated driver, so I stayed alcohol free while the others drained the bar of margaritas. Finally we got the check and were the last people to leave the restaurant. Sydney was eight, I grabbed her hand and my inebriated friends followed. Outside, the parking lot was full of police cars. My car was parked next to the only other non-police car in the parking lot. A bright light shined down on the parked car from a helicopter above. I looked around to see police armed with M-10s, expletive deleted! BettyAnne and Len seemed a little confused. I wondered if they were having flashbacks to the last days in Vietnam. I screamed, "Get in the car! " We piled into my car; the person in the vehicle next to mine was shoving little saran-wrapped packets into his mouth. I was scared and I had a car full of slightly incoherent people and an eight-year-old. I had never felt frightened, maybe nervous a few times, in Colombia or Burma. Maybe Tucson was the most dangerous place. The police waved us out of the parking lot, surely glad we were out of their way.

Lenard and BettyAnne were helping me at the show and it was going well. Then one woman dealer, I'll call her the "Barracuda," started to eye Lenard. She could see I had a pretty good setup with the certified rubies. Len laughingly told me that the Barracuda had practically put her hands into his pocket (not to fish out any spare change there). A pretty amusing scene since Len was gay and the Barracuda wasn't his type. Nevertheless Barracuda made promises to Len and Apichart that they would do better dealing with her rather than with me. I hate confrontation and didn't put up a fight. For me this was a sign to widen my gemstone horizon and start to build more of my own inventory. Luckily I had some of Apichart and Len's stuff to begin with, but I wasn't my own person under those conditions. Selling a "paper cert" wasn't the reason I got into the gem business and I was uneasy knowing there would be no secondary market for the "investors" in these stones.

Gem dealers take all sorts of risks. There were rumors of Colombian gangs hanging out in Tucson to look for unwary dealers carrying bags of precious gems. I didn't look like the typical gem dealer, but nevertheless I tried to stay aware.

Producers who put on the gem shows have little risk and a guaranteed profit. So the producers of the gem show at the Marriott decided to double their profit and put on another gem show in Tucson in September. In order to insure a space for the February show, dealers would have to participate in the September show. People from around the world love to come to Tucson in February when most of the time the temperature hovers around 70 degrees. But in September when the temperature is about 105 degrees, who would want to come? This would dilute the market in general. Mutiny ensued. A few of the insurgents, Roland Naftule, Leon Ritzler, Ray Zajicek and others held meetings at another hotel to create a new show produced by the dealers themselves. From there the American Gem Trade Association was born. Over the years AGTA took on important issues for the American gem business. Promotion of colored gemstones and defining gemstone treatment were among important contributions. In 1982 there would be a new show at the DoubleTree Hotel.

March, 1981--Reno

Since most of my gem buying was conducted with Apichart and Len in Bangkok, they wanted me to get a telex, a large metal box with typewriter keys, for instant international communication. (Email didn't exist yet.) I called around and found the company to install it. For a telex I needed a call back name (equivalent of email address). Steve and I joked around trying to think of something catchy. When the installer called to get the name, I jokingly said, "Gembitch." I really didn't mean it seriously. The guy laughed and said, "Fine," and hung up before I told him I wasn't serious about "Gembitch." So this was the birth of the Gembitch. Could I really live up to the name? Some people might know this was "tongue in cheek." On the other hand, it appeared to be edgy. The decision was made and now I had to live up to the name.

September 21, 1981--Kowloon-Hong Kong

Fall was the best time for me to go to Bangkok. The monsoons were waning and I could restock inventory for Christmas and Tucson. BettyAnne wanted to go again and suggested we stop in Hong Kong on the way. Navy nurse Lt. BettyAnne had spent R & R time in Hong Kong during the Vietnam War. We checked into a deluxe room in the brand new Regent Hotel in Kowloon. Kowloon sits on the edge of mainland China. Steep, hilly Hong Kong Island lies across the narrow channel of the harbor. A short ferry ride connected Kowloon and Hong Kong at that time. Our room had a view of the soft green waters in the harbor. I think Hong Kong was one of the most beautiful cities. Noisy with a frenetic pace, it has always been a boom town. New high-rise buildings were shooting up, surrounded by bamboo scaffolding. Ever growing and prosperous, Hong Kong was shopper's paradise. This was to be an "eat and shop" visit for two days. We had "High Tea" at the Peninsula Hotel with immaculate white table cloths and silver tea services. The British were still in charge and Hong Kong maintained a schizophrenic West meets East aura. Jet lagged, I was out in the streets at 5 a.m. I ran every morning in those days, so I would take a three-mile running tour through the streets of Kowloon. Early morning was a magical time, the streets were quietly busy with various markets awakening with exotic items: snakes, birds, ginseng, clothes, furniture and infinitely more. I loved Asia at dawn. It was always my favorite time of day. Few other crazy tourists or noisy masses were out yet. Every morning was like a rebirth of an exotic world.

Betty Anne and I took the ferry to Hong Kong Island to visit the many markets and street fairs. At that time Hong Kong was the world's most free market economy and remains so today. I found a great source of carved jade pieces at the Po Shan Jade factory. Beautiful jadeite carvings and beads were available within my budget. The more affordable carvings were multicolored with gold, light green, and gray colors. Occasionally I could find an inexpensive green or lavender piece. The carvings featured traditional designs of fruit, dragons and themes from nature that represented prosperity, profundity, and general good luck. They also sold affordable jadeite beads in soft lavender and green colors — the colors of the water in Hong Kong harbor at early morning.

September 23, 1981--Hong Kong Airport

BettyAnne insisted we fly Pan Am because they had registered nurses working on international flights. Of course in her mind this was a safer way to fly. Traveling with her constantly reminded me that she was a registered nurse. I hadn't forgotten the Larium in Burma. We checked in at the recommended time. The plane was delayed — engine issues. At 11:30 p.m. we boarded for takeoff. The airport would shut down at midnight and we had to take off, whether the plane was ready or not.

The jet geared into a quick ascent. The stewardesses (not yet called flight attendants) went through the safety procedures, the plane quieted down for the flight to Bangkok. After about a half hour--boom! A loud explosion, flames engulfed one engine. Somebody screamed that the plane was on fire. Mayhem, screaming and panic ensued. Lights went on. The pilot announced, "We are returning to Hong Kong. "There were no positive words of encouragement from the pilot. Next the stewardesses instructed us how to prepare for a crash landing. The lights dimmed to a minimum. In the near darkness the plane fell into a dead silence. Anticipation of the unknown created an aura of fear--you could smell it. BettyAnne whispered to me," Look, the stewardess is crying in the galley."She asked if I was afraid. Death itself wasn't my fear, I felt I wasn't finished yet. I still had things to do in this life. A whole litany of guilt and frustration went through my head. I'm thinking, "What a rotten mother I am, what if I die and leave my child motherless, a worthless wife leaving Steve with all that responsibility." But then maybe it wasn't my time to go. A half hour allows you to rethink a lot of things. I wasn't as afraid of dying as much as I was afraid of living irresponsibly. Time seemed interminable. Strange things flowed into my mind like the time I had a bad fall skiing at Mammoth Mountain in California. I fell about three hundred feet down a glare ice slope with my feet and skis uphill. I couldn't stop. My life did flash before me then. I wasn't injured. Scared, yes. But in that plane I had to face my guilt. But, then, you never know what is going to happen next.

Finally we landed back in Hong Kong without incident. All this trauma-drama could have been allayed if the pilot had told us that losing one engine wasn't fatal, there are other engines for backup. This I found out later. It might have been better if he even lied to us and said there were no serious problems. We went through immigration again, then we reclaimed our luggage, boarded a bus, and ended up at a crummy old hotel. BettyAnne was just pissed off. "This is where we stayed when we were on leave during the Vietnam War." What a dump!

The next crisis was that we had no idea what was next-- when would we leave? We were given no schedule, so we could not venture far from the hotel. The rooms were lousy, the food was lousy. It seemed we were being held in detention. Of course after the luxury we enjoyed in the Regent, our present digs looked even more decrepit. I assume that prison is similar to being held in an unpleasant place, not knowing when you will get out. We had no control of our immediate future. Betty Anne called Jerry who relayed the message to Steve. Steve heard the message that there was a bomb aboard, which I found out when I got home.

Two days passed. A new engine was flown in from Singapore. We proceeded back to the airport, went through all the security and immigration nonsense and flew on to Bangkok.

September 26, 1981--Bangkok

Lenard was waiting for our early morning flight. We had a couple of days in Bangkok before our next adventure. Betty Anne and I went to the silk shop to have our Thai designer wardrobe made while we were in Thailand. Yes, we had our priorities. Len planned a trip to Mae Sai, a small village near the Burma border. In spite of many interesting stones mined in Thailand, Burmese stones held much more excitement. We flew to Chiang Mai and checked into a modern new hotel. Blue and white tiles trimmed the entry. Our room was luxurious. I almost envied BettyAnne, who was going to stay in Chiang Mai, the center for handicrafts and native Thai arts while Len and I headed for the unknown, again.

The next morning Len and I drove north in a hired car with a Thai driver. We wound through the mountains of northern Thailand, passing through heavy tropical forests. Roads were paved but narrow and winding. Driving full speed we perilously avoided hitting oxcarts and working elephants — substitutes for sixteen-wheelers in this part of the world. This little trip seemed much more dangerous than the plane with the burning engine. After three hours of the harrowing drive, we stopped at a roadside stand for lunch of delicious corn fritters, the only course available. The kitchen consisted of a campfire topped with a grate for cooking. Maybe the cook had been a Girl Scout. Back in the car we went deeper into the tropical forest. Finally we arrived at a corner of the Golden Triangle. This area was one of the major border crossings with smugglers bringing heroin from Burma into Thailand which had a less restrictive atmosphere. Here the modern world met the Stone Age — Mercedes Benzes and elephant carts. Hill Tribes people came into town to sell their handicrafts and bundles of sticks in the market. A video library was there for those with electricity. Primitive life and the twentieth century existed in harmony. Had I entered an alternative universe? The market place consisted of awning-covered tables piled high with white powder substances: sugar or drugs? I didn't ask. Len and I checked into the only hotel in town. My room featured a metal bed with a thin mattress and a stained bed sheet. I hoped it had been washed. The bathroom was about 4 X 4 feet square. It was all tiled like a big shower that included a toilet and basin. How could I complain? It had plumbing. There was a four inch space under the door to the hallway. I assumed it was so the rats could easily run in and out. Nevertheless it seemed less sinister than the Strand in Rangoon. At 8 a.m. sharp, a loud horn sounded, the national anthem was played, and an elephant parade marched down the main street, the only street. Some official gave a speech in Thai. Len had a great talent for taking me to the out-of-the-way places. I had my camera with me for this incredible photo op, but the 100% humidity fogged it up--no pictures. In the oppressive heat two Hill Tribes women had opened their shirts to cool off, but nobody paid attention to the bare-breasted women.

After Len and I checked into the hotel, we asked where the border was. We walked a block away to a small river dividing Thailand and Burma. Guard houses flanked each end of a narrow foot bridge. The locals crossed the border freely. We were warned not to try to cross the river. We definitely stood out as farangs (foreigners). Nevertheless the town appeared quiet, civilized and calm. Was there an underlying danger since illicit drugs and gems supported this apparently calm village?

Len and I were invited for dinner at the home of the dealer we would be working with. We walked into a small comfortable dark wood room with a feast of at least a dozen Chinese dishes cooked by the dealer's wife. They were very gracious and spoke English fluently. The hostess apologized that there were no pork dishes. They were Muslims and pork was not allowed. We didn't miss the pork, savoring every morsel.

The dealer had made an appointment with a runner from Burma scheduled for the next morning. When we arrived for the meeting we were served tea on a shaded outdoor porch. A light breeze made it tolerable to be outside. Lukewarm green tea is usually offered at business meetings in Thailand. Since tea is a diuretic it helps to prevent your legs and feet from swelling up in the humidity and ninety-degree temperatures. Sweating is permitted. About an hour later, a large Asian finally showed up. He was at least 6'6" tall weighing maybe 220 pounds and he was not fat. Attired in an Arrow shirt and a sarong, he had hidden pockets from which he produced gemstones. Amused and totally charmed, I'm sure I stared. Again I wondered if I was on some strange planet? I guess the "bamboo telegraph "(no cell phones yet) didn't inform the sellers that I was a small buyer. The runner reached into one of the invisible pockets and pulled out a twenty-carat faceted sapphire. In spite of the poor quality of cutting the stone emitted a brilliant blue light. It was a stunner and way out of my budget. The next parcel contained large blue star sapphires, each with perfect six rayed stars. He had a parcel of peridot. Next we saw a small parcel of rubies, not of the best quality. No spinels. This meeting was set up like the ruby market in Chantaburi, where you wrote your offer on the gem paper, taped it and sent it back to the owner and awaited a counter offer. It was early afternoon when this session was over and we were to meet again the next morning to see what the counter-offers were.

Len and I dined at the only local eatery and then we turned in for an early evening. I kept thinking about the large sapphire — it had a dark blue color reminiscent of the deep part of the ocean, but didn't appear to be too dark. Regretfully I had no customer for such a stone. Before I dozed off, I realized there were few famous sapphires and virtually no named stones like large diamonds. In 1929, while Burma was still part of the empire, a sapphire rough weighing 958 carats was discovered. Described as having a superb royal blue color, it was named "Gem of the Jungle" and was cut into nine smaller stones (without names). Fine sapphires are not common on the commercial American market, many are just too dark. Sapphire should show a definite blue color even in poor lighting conditions.

The next morning Len and I returned to the dealer's home to see the results of offers. I ended up buying a small very fine green jade cabochon and some small sapphires. The jade was not quite what would be called "imperial," but it had a minor "wow" factor and it was very easy to sell.

After our meeting in Mae Sai, Len and I enjoyed another harrowing ride back to Chiang Mai. BettyAnne taunted us with all her fabulous handicraft purchases and we spent one more night in the lovely hotel before returning to Bangkok. BettyAnne and I picked up our silks and flew home.

Unfortunately several months after our trip to Mai Sae, Lenard informed me that the lovely family that we had dealt with were bombed out. Why? Were the bombers competing dealers or were they anti-Muslims? I never found out if the couple survived.

February, 1982--Tucson

AGTA produced a new show location in Tucson at the DoubleTree Hotel. I consider the first few years at the DoubleTree to have been the most fun. The dealers had left the repressive authoritarians at the Marriott. Booths were fairly small and open. This arrangement allowed dealers to get to know each other and to see what was going on and who was busy and what the hot gem items were at that show. At that time the DoubleTree had an open bar area with a piano. Gerry Manning, an opal dealer, would play the piano while dealers sat around, drank cocktails and talked. More New York dealers came to Tucson and there was a proliferation of what I called "the red, blue, and green" --the "precious stones," rubies, sapphires and emeralds. The term "semi-precious " degrades the stuff I personally found more interesting. These were referred to as "color" by some. Some tourmalines and spinel today have prices equaling many of the rubies, sapphires, and emeralds. Now we use the term "colored stones."

AGTA developed into a successful venture and grew. Eventually the show moved into the Convention Center in downtown Tucson. This was a much larger space. Booths were defined by curtains. The environment became more formal. There was no more central bar or piano around which to gather. The fun was gone. Foreign dealers started setting up booths at other shows. Many foreign dealers opened up offices in the U.S. so they could join AGTA and get into the "best" show. "Best" meaning it was well organized, aisles were open and walkable and very fine merchandise was available. Other shows often had narrow aisles and a mishmash of booths.

In the DoubleTree I had a space in the ballroom. There were other spaces in various locations in the hotel. At this point the "certified stone" business had dissipated and I had a good variety of my own gems to sell. At the first show a cart came around with freshly squeezed orange juice, sweet rolls and coffee while we were setting up. That was grand, but it didn't continue into the next show. Maybe the orange groves in Tucson were being replaced by subdivisions. The hotel had given the dealers good room rates and after the show and dinners a few dealers went to the pool for a late swim. There you could find out what was hot and what wasn't selling. The first year was good for tanzanite.

May 14, 1982--Frankfurt, Germany

BettyAnne and I decided it would be okay to bring our husbands and Sydney to Germany. They could entertain each other while we shopped. We rented a car at the Frankfurt airport and Steve was the driver. We headed for Idar-Oberstein and managed to get in a minor crash with a British Army truck. The British were driving on the wrong side of the road this time. Germans drive on the right side like the rest of the non-British world. We had a reservation at the Sonnehof (sun house) in Veitsrodt about three miles from Idar. When we booked this trip we didn't know this was prime feasting time in southwest Germany. White asparagus and fresh strawberries were in season and our hotel chef served them with great reverence. In this area of Germany there are patches of the Schwartzwald (Black

Forest) and patches of farm land with newer homes. Northern Europeans have large windows in their homes, as did the Sonnehof, to capture the somewhat rare sunlight.

The Sonnehof had an indoor swimming pool. Sydney and Steve always brought their swimming suits when we traveled. (Sydney still clings to this habit no matter where she goes.)I decided to take Sydney to the pool. On the door to the pool were many handwritten notes all written in German. Ignorant of what they said I opened the door and found two men swimming nude. Quickly I closed the door and wondered what was appropriate. A while later Steve took Sydney to the pool when no one else was there. I never returned to the pool because I was unsure about all those unreadable messages. Were there certain hours for men only?

The next day we drove in Idar to shop. BettyAnne and Jerry went shopping for beads. German beads were cut from the best materials and were quite expensive. The Germans cut beads from a variety of gem materials that weren't cut at that time by Asian bead cutters. In the nineteenth century the Germans staked out gem material sites in Africa and Brazil and had managed to monopolize some of the best rough material.

Steve, Sydney and I went to Gerhardt Becker's shop. Herr Becker designed carved art pieces from gem materials, especially quartz and tourmaline. These pieces were completed with 18K gold details. His subjects included birds, animals and flowers. That day he gave us a rather formal lecture on the history of engraved gems. Stone carvings date back thousands of years. In the Bronze Age finely carved gem materials were used as stamp seals to create signatures on official documents and to seal storage jars. Besides being functional items, these seals were worn as power objects for protection and good fortune. In the first and second centuries Romans established one of their most northern outposts in Trier, Germany bringing their technologies and culture with them. Did the all the Romans retreat to Rome during the fall of the Roman Empire or did they stay in the verdant valleys of Germany and continue their arts and crafts?

The following day Herr Becker took us to Trier to see the fortress remains of the Romans. What an honor for us! Becker was born in the 1930s. He was a young teen during the war. One day he was riding his bicycle across an open field trying to avoid being seen by Allied planes dropping bombs in the area. At the end of WWII he was forced to forage throughout the German countryside to find food. Traveling through western Germany we saw many modern buildings and many war ruins which still remained at that time. How much was destroyed in the two world wars? All this destruction in Europe is hard to imagine today.

Elsewhere in the world what is being destroyed now? What madness we humans can create.

The five of us departed from the gourmet meals of white asparagus at the Sonnehof and drove on through wine country German style. Along the Mosel and Rhine rivers vineyards covered the sloping hills. We stopped at the ancient village of Bernkastel Kues and walked through narrow streets designed for horses, not cars, to visit the wine tasting rooms. Next stop--Luxembourg. The city center appeared to be in the fifteenth century with tall Gothic spires everywhere. We found a champagne tasting room. The five of us sat down and the server set out five glasses and poured in the champagne. We all started to laugh, as Sydney was eight. We drank her portion while she pouted.

Finally we drove to Geneva where Christie's auction house was holding an "Important Jewelry Auction." It was to be held in the very grand Hotel Richemond (rich world). Certainly this was a new world to us, a venue where the truly wealthy shop and entertain themselves. The auction room was decorated in an elegant Victorian style — flocked red wallpaper, gilt wherever possible, and lighted with extravagant crystal chandeliers. Soon it filled with elegantly dressed Europeans. One woman overpowered the room with the scent of "Joy", the most expensive perfume. I became slightly nauseated . The auctioneer called out bids in both French and in English. "Important Jewelry" translates to be expensive pieces made with gold or platinum and set mostly with diamonds, rubies, emeralds and sapphires.

Some of Christie's auctions feature "Magnificent Jewelry" with pieces boasting a royal history and parures (sets of jewelry with matching necklaces, earrings and bracelets). Sets were constructed with matching emeralds or matching rubies trimmed with many carats of smaller diamonds as accents to the colored gemstones. Extravagant diamond tiaras might be included in a "Magnificent Jewelry" auction. Obviously there are some pretty fancy parties being thrown somewhere in a world unknown to most of us.

The auction continued the next day featuring much cheaper pieces. I put a bid in for an 18K yellow gold watch and got it for $300 USD. Steve, BettyAnne, Jerry and Sydney spent the day shopping for fancy chocolates. Geneva's chocolatiers create art in the form of edible candies. I think it was healthier for me to stay at the jewelry auction.

- Lesson eleven: When economic markets get out of control beware of potential bad investments (like gemstones). They are nice to collect, not "invest."

- Lesson twelve: Switzerland has fabulous ice cream and chocolates. Dieters beware!

## Chapter 8 - MAJOR CHANGES

December 7, 1982--Frankfurt

Once more I took the train to Idar-Oberstein from Frankfurt--this time I knew how to change the trains. I needed inventory for the Tucson show in February. The Barracuda had made her moves on the boys from Bangkok. She promised to do many wonderful things for Len and Apichart. And what was I going to do? To avoid some sort of cat fight I decided find my own niche in the gem business. I could still go to Bangkok and get my own gems. I talked to Steve about going to Germany to buy for the Tucson show. He said he was fine with my traveling even though it was close to Christmas.

One time Fred stated, "Fine quality amethyst is one of the most beautiful gemstones and should really cost more." True, but amethyst is not rare, so the price remains at the lower end. The best amethyst shows a deep violet color, but not too dark, with rich red overtones. This week in Idar-Oberstein amethyst was my favorite stone. Gems seem to bring out an extreme fickleness in me. Amethyst would become my specialty — for a while anyway.

A fine layer of snow covered the quiet streets of Idar-Oberstein. The humidity created a chill I wasn't used to. Reno could be very cold and snowy, but never with the bone-chilling dampness of European winters. I stayed at the Schwann Hotel in central Idar. Close by was an affordable restaurant that served pork medallions with a bearnaise sauce. Naturally they served French fries. Maybe it was the French fries that attracted me to Europe. A local Nahe white wine (middle-not too dry, not too sweet) accompanied this feast. This became my routine for the week.

The great amethyst hunt began. German cutters had excellent sources of African and Brazilian rough and they cut them for their maximum beauty. So I visited Herr Becker to get his referrals of who would have the best stones. He graciously took me to several cutters with good amethyst selections. Fortunately amethyst forms in a range

94

of sizes, so I bought stones ranging from five to twenty carats.

Then Becker advised me that a display of all violet gems would be boring and he was right. A good display needs contrast. Mexican fire opal was his suggestion — it is very colorful and would create a striking contrast with the amethyst. This transparent material was cut into faceted stones. Some were displayed in color lines with several stones displayed in a row with colors ranging from a pale yellow gradating to an intense orange. Brilliant idea! A few stones were bi-colors, yellow on one end, orange on the other. These unusual bi-colors would be easy to sell. Bright red stones were also available. This selection of fire opal lacked the play of color (that internal rainbow found in opals) usually associated with Australian opal. It was transparent with very bright yellows, oranges, and reds in an affordable price range. With plenty of violet and orange booty I returned home after five days.

December 13, 1982

Upon my arrival home I found Steve was gone. The tall body that Steve inhabited was still at home, but somebody else was living in the body. This person, whoever he was, was angry at my leaving at this time of the year. He didn't have Steve's sense of humor. I was baffled. He was forgetful, and would forget how to shift his car. He rejected my suggestion to see a doctor. He had grown up with a religious dogma that he had suddenly rediscovered and doctors were out of the question. He would pray. I left for the Gem Show not knowing what was going on with Steve.

February, 1983--Tucson

Vivid violet and outrageous orange dominated my display for the show. My clothes were violet and orange, bright but tasteful. This was the eighties and everything was bright and oversized and over the top. My manicurist painted my fingernails orange and violet. I had streaks of orange and violet dyed into my hair. On the flight to Tucson I changed planes in Phoenix. As I waited for the plane change, some guy was giving me really strange looks--I had forgotten about the streaks in my hair. At the show I got varied comments on the whole orange-violet scheme, but most were laughingly favorable. Len's new young boyfriend gushed, "I love your hair." The fire opal went well; there hadn't been a lot of fire opal in the show before. The availability of fire opal has always been irregular. Some years there is an abundance of some materials and at other times they are hard to find. The bicolors sold right away and the color lines did well. Successful show! The amethyst sold well, but the more unusual fire opal overpowered the more common amethyst. Maybe the market was opening up to more unusual stones.

Over the year I found a source of amethyst roughfrom Namibia to be cut in Bangkok. The Namibian rough was always small but the color was strong, so they were cut into calibrated sizes, mostly rounds but some into fancy shapes like hexagons, half moons, and pear shapes.

Calibrated stones are cut to fit standard manufactured mountings. For example: 2, 3, 4, 5 mm. rounds, 5 X 3, 6 X 4, 7 X 5 mm. ovals and so forth. (6 mm. is the equivalent of ¼ inch.) These save the jeweler time and hence the customer money. If the stones are "free" sizes, then custom mountings must be made by hand which adds to the cost.

The gem market is somewhat fluid and constantly changing. A year or so later the Namibian mine was sold and I lost this source of amethyst rough. Next I found a source of small rough from Mauritius. Then I found a source of larger rough from Brazil and Uruguay. These were cut into beautiful larger stones that were very saleable. Unfortunately when I bought the second lot of large rough from the same dealer, that rough had been "blasted" in the mining process. Blasting created cracks in the stones, making them essentially worthless. I confronted the dealer from whom I had purchased the rough from. He just shrugged and I took the loss. I was not knowledgeable enough to know the fine points of buying rough. That created more risk for me. The whole process was another learning curve.

Back home Steve was getting more forgetful. Since he wouldn't listen to my pleas to go to a doctor, we decided to send him to his mother in Southern California. When I took him to the airport he had difficulty making it to the appropriate gate. We sat down to rest a couple of times. Finally he flew off. Within a few days his mother put him into a Christian Science rest home. He was blind. He never saw a doctor. He didn't leave the rest home alive. The death certificate stated the cause of death as a cancerous brain tumor. He was 40 years old.

Summer, 1983

Widowhood is heartbreaking and liberating at the same time. Sydney attended a year-round school and had four weeks of vacation between each quarter. She visited her grandmother in Newport Beach and I tried to manage things at home. Steve had had a business and there were matters I had to resolve. Fortunately he had a business associate who just continued his appraisal business and I did my best with the rest of the loose ends.

Strange stuff occurred during this summer. One evening I was leaving my fifth floor office to go to dinner with my parents. It was about 6 p.m. and the building was deserted. I stepped into the elevator, pressed the down button, the doors closed, something snapped, and the elevator went into free fall. Then it stopped. Was it going to continue to plummet? For about a half hour I sat on the floor trying not to move and wondered if this was the end for me. My parents were probably wondering where I was. Worry mode took over. Finally I started to yell, "Get me out of here. "The cleaning crew had just arrived. Half an hour later, the police rescue unit arrived and broke into the ceiling of the elevator and pulled me out. The elevator was stuck between floors. As I was assisted to the next floor up, I looked down in the emptiness of the shaft. It was a long drop down, but I didn't go there. For a year or so afterwards, I took the stairs.

A memorial fund was raised to buy an art piece in Steve's name for the local art museum. The museum backed up to the Truckee River in an older house in a tree shaded neighborhood. It was a hot July day and I had a donation to drop off. I parked my car under the biggest shade tree a few houses down from the museum. When I returned to my car an old man came out to tell me I could not park there. As it was legal street parking and I had only been parked for a few minutes, I protested as I got into the car. The driver's side window was open. He reached in and hit me on the nose. Blood gushed from my nose and I started to cry. I had not been obnoxious. I merely justified what was perfectly right and legal. Was the whole universe in a conspiracy against me? I felt I was being punished and victimized by some unknown force. I was overcome by a strange sense of paranoia. When I got home I called the museum and told them what had happened. They wanted me to press assault charges. This man had harassed many other people, but no one filed any complaints. I did press charges. It was time to stop this nut case. We went to court about three months later and he was convicted on a minor offense.

Grief manifests itself in a variety of ways. I suffered hair loss. My dress size dropped from a size 12 to a size 6. During this time I wondered where the bottom of this cycle was. But self-pity is not a solution to any issue. I had to move on with my life. With the weight loss I had to get a whole new wardrobe, which was not a bad thing—just expensive. Finally feeling my sense of independence, I cut my fairly long hair into a pixie cut I could manage more easily. It was time for a full life make-over.

In spite of my new-found paranoia and sense of loss, a new attitude lifted the spirit of the country after the economic troubles of 1979-1981. Interest rates had dropped and hard asset investments waned. Fortunately certified gemstones lost any luster they may have had as other investments promised greater potential. The age of excess in fashion had begun. Women's clothes suddenly grew shoulder pads, power suits were the new norm for career women, big hair proliferated, and pearls dominated the jewelry market. Jewelry was an important part of the fashion scene with colored stone jewelry increasing in popularity. Now gemstones were being purchased to fulfill their traditional role of personal adornment. I was ready to reassess and move forward.

July 29, 1981--London The Royal Wedding

World events can create fashion trends. This was the day of the "Wedding of the Century" for Lady Diana Spencer and Prince Charles. Worldwide viewers saw the wedding party with all the female royal family members decked out in pearls. Undoubtedly some of these strands of pearls were natural "oriental" pearls fished from the Persian Gulf. Or they could have been Akoya pearls cultured in Japan. The giant pearls from the South Seas hadn't hit the mass market yet; these would have been astronomically expensive, but a few of the wealthy British sported large pearls that could only be from the South Seas. Queen Elizabeth wore multistrands of pearls layering into 28 to 30 inch lengths. The Queen Mother sported strands about 48 to 50 inches in length. (I assume these two queens had pearls from the Persian Gulf.) Younger women wore chokers. It was obvious the older the wearer, the longer the pearl strands were. Suddenly there was a boom in the Akoya cultured pearls from Japan. The cultured pearl market was centered in Japan at this time. These pearls were predominantly white in color, spherical, and very traditional (and very boring).

Shellfish like oysters create pearls when irritants inhabit them. Pearls are essentially nature's way of creating a "scab" around a grain of sand or small worm that penetrates the shell of a mollusk. The nacre that grows in layers around the irritant produces the pearly luster. Pearls have always had an important role in the quest for gems. They, too, drove the exploration of the world to find new sources. The Persian Gulf was an early source of pearls for the Romans and eventually the Europeans. Since natural pearls were the rarest of the gem materials, they were the most valued and most expensive. After the European known world was expanded by Columbus, new sources of pearls were discovered. After all, Columbus was sailing all over in search of wealth: it was not a mapping expedition. Cortez discovered pearl sources in the Gulf of California. Exploration of the Pacific Ocean opened up new pearl sources around Tahiti, the Philippines, Malaysia, and in Australia.

As a lover of art, museums and pearls, I once spent a day in the Prado Museum in Madrid just looking at the Dutch Renaissance portrait paintings of women wearing pearls. Most of them wore pearl drop earrings that would be the envy of women today. Queen Elizabeth I of England was always portrayed wearing her wealth of pearls. Pearls trimmed her hair, were sewed into her clothing, and hung in many strands around her neck. Indian Maharajas (men) wore so many pearls they outdid even the opulent Elizabeth.

Since natural pearls were so rare, in the 1890s Kokichi Mikimoto began to experiment with planting a seed bead into Akoya oysters that inhabited the waters around Japan. Eventually several beads were planted in each oyster, then mesh bags of oysters were dropped back into the sea for a couple of years. Cultured pearls were born. Mussels growing in Lake Biwa, Japan had similar good results. Freshwater cultured pearls in colors of peach, pink, white, mauves and gold are readily available on today's market. They are very affordable for jewelry. Pearls when worn around the neck have a warm sensuous feeling. They take on one's body heat—what's not to love about pearls!

September 21, 1983--Narita, Japan

From one of the trade magazines I found a pearl company in Kobe. I had a small life insurance settlement and decided to invest in pearls. One day in Tokyo acclimated me to a new culture. I wandered around looking at the glass and concrete city. In spite of heavy traffic the

Japanese are quiet and polite. Every restaurant window featured wax food models, works of art in themselves. Large department stores displayed luxury items. To pass time I rode the immaculate but very crowded subway. Then I went to the train station to plan my journey to Kobe.

The next day I boarded the bullet train to Kobe. It was filled with permed Japanese business men. Apparently curly hair was the current fashion. The bullet moved along smoothly and it was nice to enjoy the speed and comfort. No cramped seating like the plane.

I had telexed the pearl dealer that I was coming. He suggested I stay at a very new modern hotel which faced the bay in Kobe. For our meeting the dealer had sent a driver. A white-haired Japanese man who spoke the Queen's English picked me up. He told me he was born in Australia to people culturing pearls in the tropical waters of northeast Australia. When World War II broke out, his family was forced to leave Australia and they came back to Japan. Before the war Kobe's buildings were wooden structures. The U.S. forces fire-bombed Kobe and the entire city burned to the ground. Now the city had regrown into a beautiful modern metropolis with a stunning bay view. Once more I thought about the destruction of the war and then rebirth. These ideas never crossed my mind at home. Somehow life after destruction can occur in a beautiful way on this planet.

The pearl dealer, Mr. Shinoda, met us at the door of his office. He greeted me with a formal bow. I removed my shoes and went into a carpeted room. Mr. Shinoda graciously told me I was his first female client and he apologized that he could not treat me as he treated his male customers. This meant no geisha houses after we did business. I was amused and flattered. In this male-dominated business, I just wanted to be treated fairly. I was here for the pearls-- not going to the geisha house was not a problem.

He asked me what kind of merchandise I was looking for. My clientele would buy a good quality in the middle price range. Then his helpers laid out about a hundred hanks of pearls on the floor. A hank consists of several pearl strands that have the same quality factors: size, shape, blemishes, luster, and color. We sat on the floor and I examined every strand. All the pearls I looked at were locally grown in Akoya oysters. Size generally ranged from 4 to 8 mm. Rarely, 9 to 10 mm. pearls occur. Shapes were mostly spherical, but some were baroque (misshapen). Minor blemishes on pearls lower the price, but once strung, blemishes are less noticeable. Strands that aren't perfectly spherical, but not noticeably misshapen, have considerably lower prices. To me luster, the rich surface quality, is the most important factor in the pearl's beauty. The surface should have deep shine, never be dull. Colors of Akoya range from white to pale yellow. Pink overtones in white pearls are considered the best color. I examined every strand and found a good assortment. After I made my selections he told me I had a good eye for pearls. Of course, he would not have said anything else. The driver took me back to the hotel. Mr. Shinoda arranged to have me picked up for dinner. His wife would join us. To him this was an acceptable substitute for entertainment. I was happy. We went to a particular restaurant that allowed women. Mr. Shinoda ordered the eel. It was not my favorite meal but this was considered "special" and I appreciated the honor.

One challenge in Kobe for me was the Asian toilets. These were in places that did not cater to western tourists. I had seen some in Thailand. They consisted of rather small holes placed at floor level. The severe squat challenged my western legs. Maybe these have some advantages in the area of sanitation. One must adapt when traveling. Laugh and enjoy.

The next day I met with Mr. Shinoda to look at the invoice and had money wired to him from my bank. We took a tour of Kobe. Dinner this night was to include a couple of American Japanese who were born in Chicago and had moved to Japan. We went to a family-style restaurant with Japanese style barbecued chicken. In spite of the fact that this was new protocol for Mr. Shinoda, we all had a good time.

September 24, 1983--Bangkok

High interest rates in the American economy had dropped and hard asset investments dried up. Gemstone and gold investments had lost their luster. The 1980s began a flashy fashion period. Jewelry was now a big fashion item. I started to have jewelry made in Bangkok. Apichart put together a studio with good jewelers. Mr. Ming, Apichart's right hand man, would take my jewelry orders first thing. This was more critical than going to the silk shop first. I had all these lovely gemstones and a growing jewelry clientele at home. My pieces consisted mostly of one-of- a-kind pieces using a variety of colored stones. Fine rubies and sapphires were generally too expensive for my pieces. Sometimes I could find a pretty fancy colored sapphire and put together a nice piece that was affordable. My clients at home were working women looking for something more unusual than mass-produced jewelry found in the local stores. I still bought stones for the Tucson show. Apichart's factory was cutting a variety of gemstones. I always liked to find spinel, exotic colored zircon, and whatever was beautiful, saleable and affordable.

December 22, 1983--Bangkok

I decided to take Sydney to Bangkok for Christmas. At age 10, this was her first Christmas without her father. As a special treat we flew business class on Japan Air Lines, so we luxuriated in larger seats and enjoyed better airline food. We stayed at Len's house. David Dikinis, another dealer from Los Angeles, was also at Len's house. When I took Sydney to Apichart's office, she was immediately whisked away by one of Apichart's staff and I didn't see her until the end of the day. She was ecstatic. She had been taken down to the street and she had a whole fried fish wrapped in newspaper for lunch. Obviously she had fun that day, no complaints from her. Apichart invited Sydney to go on his Christmas gift to his employees — a boat trip down the River Kwai for three days. I was not invited. She seemed pretty excited so I let her go. She was also a good swimmer. Her vision was that this would be a trip on a luxury liner. When she returned from the trip she expressed her disappointment. The boat was a large wooden covered raft with a hole in the back for a toilet. Now she looks back on it as an "adventure." When I got home people were shocked that I had allowed her to go. I knew these Thais and trusted them to take care of her. Two days before New Year's Eve, Lenard's brother died and Lenard left for Reno. I finished my business without him. New Year's Eve David bought a bunch of fireworks and he and Sydney spent the evening shooting rockets and generally disturbing the neighborhood. We left to go to Japan for more pearls on January 2.

January 2, 1984--Osaka, Japan

The first night, we stayed in Osaka. We went to dinner at the hotel at a teppanyaki bar. I had warned Sydney not to order beef, because it was terribly expensive. The menu was bi-lingual and it was beef or nothing. She fidgeted until I said, "Order the beef." All the food was grilled in front of us. Fresh garlic, carrots, the debated beef, all smothered in a delicious sauce.

I wasn't aware that New Year was the biggest holiday time in Japan. Based on the indigenous Shinto religion, a kami (god) enters one's house on the new year. Preparation for this event means a thorough house cleaning and plans for feasting.

Mr. Shinoda again was very gracious and Sydney and I were invited to his home to celebrate in the traditional festivities. Mr. Shinoda had three children bracketing Sydney's age. The family was all dressed in tradition kimonos. Food was prepared before the holiday and put into bento boxes. Sydney was totally taken with the little dried fish from the boxes. I began to worry that she was developing very exotic tastes that couldn't be satisfied when we got home. The next day we visited Shinto temples with the Shinodas. There was a light dusting of snow on the ground. The high humidity made it feel as cold as an August day in San Francisco. Finally the holiday was over and I went to Mr. Shinoda's office to fondle more pearls.

- Lesson thirteen: We all go through some rough periods in our lives. We can survive these times.

## Chapter 9 - UNEXPECTED CHANGES

February, 1984

Change dominated this year, both good and not so good. Out of the blue everything I depended on for my business turned upside down.

First the killer struck: a new synthetic amethyst hit the gem market. At first the Gemological Institute of America said there was no way to distinguish synthetic amethyst from natural material. That killed the amethyst market. With the GIA's attitude, the amethyst buyer couldn't be sure what he was buying. With this uncertainty, my amethyst inventory languished.

Synthetic amethyst presented a crisis for me. I was heavily invested in these natural violet stones. At Tucson I bought a bunch of synthetic stones to take home to my lab to examine. There had to be a difference between the synthetics and natural stones. Nature doesn't work in a laboratory; more complex factors go into the creation of gem materials in nature. After weeks of viewing the natural stones microscopically, I finally immersed the stones in water to view color zoning which is visible in large amethyst. When immersed in water, color zoning is easy to discern. Then I examined all the synthetic stuff under the microscope. I discovered a subtle difference! Natural gemstones form in particular ways, the synthetic material forms differently. The immersed natural amethyst exhibits geometric color zoning with hexagonal angles; these angles resemble the points on an amethyst crystal (six sides forming into a sharp point). Natural amethyst crystals show colorless, pinkish or yellow zones along with strong violet zones. Synthetic amethyst does not have these varied color hexagonal zones. The synthetic material had wispy inclusions not found in the natural stuff. I set up a little demonstration at the Tucson show to show to buyers the subtle difference between the natural amethyst and the synthetic. A young woman, Cheryl Kremkow, came in to see the demonstration. She was a journalist and lived in San Francisco at that time. We became friends and a year or so later she moved to Hong Kong. I stayed with her in Hong Kong a few times. She was responsible for introducing me to saag paneer (spicy spinach and cheese) and nan (a flat bread) — I'm eternally grateful for that!

Finally the GIA came out with their own method of distinguishing the natural from the synthetic. But the market had already gone to hell, my investment with it.

\*\*\*\*\*\*\*\*\*\*\*\*\*\*\*\*\*\*\*\*\*

At the Tucson show Roland Naftule, president of the American Gem Trade Association, asked me to join the board of directors. Of course, I thought this was absolutely wonderful — such a privilege. On second thought, what were the board members thinking? Didn't they know that I was opinionated and outspoken? Maybe they thought I would nod in agreement or maybe I would be the token blond. Tact has never been in my skill set. In 1984 I hadn't learned restraint about my opinions. (Fortunately as I have aged, I have learned not to express every thought.) As the only woman, at times I felt as though I was in a room with a bunch of bullies. Bullies bring out my toughest side — I get defensive, even though most of the time I try to avoid conflict. But as time went on I just didn't know how to deal with this group. I was an outsider and maybe I felt intimidated. I'm sure I was the only monolingual person on the board. Compared to these guys I was a bit provincial.

For me this was a challenge that would open my eyes to a world I had yet to experience – the illusion of power. Nevertheless this was a great honor.

Then the biggest shake-up occurred. I got a late night phone call from Lenard. He was calling from Hong Kong, where he and Apichart had fled. Interest rates in Thailand had been raised from a usurious rate of 24% to an outrageous rate of 36%. Many Thai gem dealers fled the country when they were unable to meet the steep interest payments. One of Apichart's creditors had come to his office with a machete to kill him. Yes, it can be a rough business! Fortunately Apichart had time to hide in the basement and escaped the attempted assassination. Then he and Lenard escaped to Hong Kong. At the time I was having amethyst rough cut in Apichart's factory. I had become dependent on Lenard to handle the import and export paperwork required by the Thai government. My work wouldn't get done without Len. I needed to find other alternatives. My business would stall out at this point if couldn't find a substitute cutter and jewelry manufacturer somewhere. Bangkok dominated the cutting market at this time. With a sense of desperation, I had to go on the hunt for new people.

March 12, 1984--Singapore

My friend, Liz Summers, had spare time and money and was ready to travel, so we booked Singapore Airlines and flew the long way to Bangkok. Singapore Airlines had the best service and ambience. As you boarded the plane you could smell the fragrant wash cloths readied for the first food service. The attendant staff dressed in navy blue long skirts and tunic tops; they were exceptionally attentive and gracious. The bad news was that we were on a longer flight schedule that included a stop in Singapore, extending our travel time an additional twelve hours.

Singapore is a small city state located on the tip of the Malaysian Peninsula. It's prosperous and exceptionally clean and is run by a benevolent dictator. There was no trash along the streets, unlike in Bangkok or Hong Kong. Laws here are very strict and you would be in big trouble if you spit gum out on the sidewalk. We had a several-hour layover here so we took a taxi into the city center. A thriving business center, Singapore has modern skyscrapers and amenities. We lunched at the historic Raffles Hotel and walked through an outdoor market and modern shops. Singapore was more modern-western in appearance without the strong Asian feel that distinguished Bangkok or Hong Kong.

March 12, 1984--Bangkok

Liz and I stayed downtown at the Royal Orchid Hotel located on the Chao Phyra river. We could walk down to the gem center on Mahaesak Street which paralleled New Road. I had a couple of kilos of small amethyst rough from Namibia. Small calibrated amethyst was still selling. The price of the calibrated stones was not affected by the proliferation of the synthetic amethyst. The rough consisted of small pieces, but the color was a deep rich violet.

I was on my own. I knew the neighborhood and had to visit each shop to find a new cutter. I had some leads but nothing concrete. One of my leads took me to an American ex-pat with a cutting shop. He was so rude to me that I left in disgust. I have never been treated rudely by any foreign dealer in the business before or since.

I began knocking on doors around Mahaesak Street where most of the gem cutters worked. Since this area of Bangkok catered to foreign buyers, most of the cutters spoke English, the international business language. I found another cutter who would cut my rough and ship it to me. After one month I received the finished stones that had been cut into very tiny calibrated pieces. I wanted larger stones that were more saleable. The cutter charged by the piece; he justified the cutting by saying he cut it so it was all flawless. Microscopic inclusions would not make larger stones less saleable for this inexpensive amethyst. But the cutter made a lot more money by charging for the more numerous smaller stones. Here was another tough lesson I hadn't foreseen.

Obviously I didn't find a satisfactory, dependable cutter on that trip. It was time to rethink what inventory I could sell. Lenard and Apichart were people I could trust. Trust was the most important thing for my business. Once you find good people to work with, you continue to do your business with them. What would my alternatives be? The life of a gem dealer is a crap shoot. You can't win if you don't play — but you could still lose.

Late Spring, 1984--San Juan, Puerto Rico

With many air miles accumulated on my frequent flyer card, I booked a free flight to Puerto Rico. I had heard that some large jewelry chains manufactured jewelry there. Feeling panicked about losing Bangkok as my business support, I desperately thought maybe I could find a jewelry manufacturer in San Juan. Of course I had no leads or any real knowledge of where or how this was being done in Puerto Rico. So I wandered the streets like a lost soul in search of some place that manufactured. No one knew what I was looking for, but a few of the locals warned me to be very careful. Apparently muggings were common. And maybe I didn't look like I belonged there. After three days of walking around on the streets and finally on the beach, I realized this was a hopeless venture and flew home contemplating my next step. Hadn't I learned something on my trip to Bogota?

Summer, 1984--Phillipsburg, Montana

I had met a guy in Tucson who was selling sapphire rough from Montana. He had a setup in Bangkok to heat the rough and then have it cut. There are two major sapphire deposits in Montana: Missouri River and Yogo Gulch. The Yogo Gulch material is tied up exclusively by a corporation. Yogo Gulch produces beautiful brilliant medium dark blue sapphires, but they are usually quite small, a carat or less. The Missouri River rough is alluvial material found in a range of pastel colors, greens, blues, pinks, and oranges. Unfortunately most of the stones are an insipid medium green color. So taking another risk, once more I jumped into unknown territory. I arranged to go Phillipsburg, Montana with this guy. He knew a nice old miner who had buckets of the pastel sapphire rough. I bought two kilograms of rough which should yield about two thousand carats of finished stones. Since this is alluvial material, most of the rough is rounded water-worn pebbles; these shapes make the material ideal for cutting. Rounded pebbles will give you pretty good yield if they are cut into round faceted stones. The small rough stones ranged from about a half to almost one full gram. There are five carats to a gram; cut yield of round pebbles should be about 20%. Consequently, most of the finished stones weighed less than one carat. When I got home I sorted the rough as to color and noted the percentage of each color that I expected to get back when the stones were cut. Then I sent the rough to the guy so he could get them finished in Bangkok. In Bangkok the rough would first be heat treated (burned). Burning the rough clarifies it, burning out any rutile inclusions that might be in them. Burning also intensifies the color (most of the time). A couple of months later when I received the finished goods there was a smaller percentage of pinks and oranges than I had calculated from the untreated rough. Much of the Missouri River material is color zoned giving me some bi-colored stones. Unlike bi-colored tourmalines the bi-colored sapphires were not very attractive. So I called the guy and complained about the apparent shortage of pink and orange stones. He told me that when they treated the rough the colors had probably changed and that there was no possibility that the material could have been switched or tampered with. Of course I will never really know, but I didn't believe him. Also I had no idea what could have happened at the cutting factory. Once more I found that I needed to find people that I could trust so I could be sure that my interests were part of their business ethics.

That year felt like I was living the "perils of Pauline." I tried not to think of myself as a victim.

- Lesson fourteen: Finding people you can trust in the gem business is essential. How to find them out of the blue is a big challenge or just dumb luck.

- Lesson fifteen: Realizing you can't control outside forces is a lesson especially hard for control freaks.

- Lesson sixteen: When the universe seemingly craps on your head, you need to clean up the mess first. Then you need to find a new universe.

- Lesson seventeen: Sometimes life provides you with a trial and error philosophy. It's part of the learning curve.

# Chapter 10 - AGTA

February 1985--Tucson

National news featured a story about a jeweler being sued by a client who bought an expensive emerald. The client discovered that the emerald had been treated. For many years, probably centuries, emeralds have been soaked in oil which permeates the minute fractures in the stone. Consequently the emerald would appear to have improved clarity, the internal fractures would be less apparent. There's nothing new about stone treatment. Two thousand years ago the Romans dyed banded agate material to be cut into cameos. Rusty iron pieces were used to turn the banded agates into orange and white pieces. Burning some gemstones intensified their color, also an ancient treatment. The problem was no one had informed the public about stone treatment.

Since treatment issues were swirling about, I had a sign made for the Tucson show for my Montana sapphire stock. It stated in capital letters "MONTANA SAPPHIRES— GUARANTEED HEAT TREATED." For me the sign was satire; it was supposed to make the buyers laugh and maybe think and question. It was time to clarify issues about treatment. Informing the jeweler and the consumer about treatment became necessary. It was the honest thing to do. And in the long run it would protect dealers from future blow backs. Treatment isn't about deceptive practices, it's about creating the most beautiful product. Irradiated blue topaz was becoming a popular gemstone. The transformation of an uninteresting colorless topaz into a brilliant striking blue color was just the forefront of treatments to enhance natural materials into more attractive and marketable products. Buyers were amused by my heating declaration. It seemed time to open up the conversation about gem treatment.

In spite of having my Montana sapphire inventory displaying many stones with insipid medium green colors, there were some pretty oranges and pinks that sold well. Even some of the less spectacular colors sold. My investment was not great, so I could sell them at reasonable prices. The buyers, who were mostly jewelers, didn't seem to care about the stated heat treatment. This was a matter of informative messaging, not a warning about quality or desirability. After the prior year I felt fortunate to have any inventory at all.

1984-86 The AGTA Thing — Phoenix-New York-Dallas.

Board membership was an opportunity to observe power in action. The other board members had much more experience than I had and they were the "good old boys." At first "insecurity" was my middle name. But I had created a gem business and my meager experiences did give me insight into the workings of the business. And I had been invited by the AGTA president.

The first year I learned that board activities were self-perpetuating. One meeting the board would enact certain situations and rules. The next meeting would be about rescinding all the issues that came up in the prior meeting. Then on the third meeting all the issues that were affirmed in the first meeting would be re-enacted. A bloody perpetual motion machine!

Power is a perception--nobody really walks on water or parts the sea. Power is an illusion that is held by the masses. Being quiet during meetings, then occasionally saying something intelligent makes one look very powerful. Holding back makes others think you already know what's going on, even though you may be totally clueless. (I was definitely intimidated by the other board members at first.)In the meetings I kept reminding myself that all of us put pants on one leg at a time. I tried to behave.

The issue of gemstone treatment came up at every meeting. So where was the debate? Gemstone treatment can create more beautiful stones. This was not a plot to deceive. It can be compared to women putting on makeup. In textiles, dyes and treatments are used to make a more attractive product. There was no reason to keep gemstone treatments a secret.

Gem treatments are common in the gem world. Some of them have been done for centuries. Dyeing can be done to stones that are porous. Ancient Romans perfected dyeing chalcedony. Black onyx does not exist in nature. Gray chalcedony is boiled in a sugar solution, then soaked in sulfuric acid; the result is an opaque black stone that is commonly used in jewelry. Other gem materials that can be dyed include turquoise and jadeite. Jadeite can be dyed a deep lavender color or an intense green. This treatment is difficult to detect.

Heat is the most common treatment. Heat can lighten or alter the color of certain gems: tourmaline, topaz, aquamarine, amethyst, rubies, and sapphires. Commercial citrines come from amethyst that has been heated. Heating also burns out inclusions in some gems, especially rubies and sapphires.

Various forms of nuclear bombardment can alter a gemstone's color. As with the Deepdene, diamonds can be irradiated and heated to create blues, greens, yellows, and occasionally other colors. Commercial blue topaz has been irradiated and heated. Natural blue topaz exists, but it has a pale insipid color.

Oiling or resin treatment is used on emeralds to disguise internal fractures.

Impregnation is common for turquoise. A plastic or wax substance is forced into the porous gem material. This prevents the turquoise from becoming "dingy" from absorbing body oils.

One day we board members were all sitting around a large rectangular dark wood table, I don't remember the city, just the table. I made a motion about declaring gem treatment. The motion for some reason seemed confusing, so I explained it. President Ray Zajicek, an emerald dealer, liked the motion after analyzing it. Maurice Shire, a preeminent emerald dealer shouted at me, "People like you don't even belong in this business." I guess I pushed his buttons a bit. What did "like you" really mean? That I was inexperienced, WASPY, blond--or did he think I was stupid? I sat and looked at him. He probably thought I would cry. I had heard a lot worse from my father and my mother-in-law and sat unfazed by his outburst. The others remained silent for a moment.

What I learned from this exchange was when someone reacts strongly, it's often because the other person is right in what he or she said and the reactor didn't like it. That's politics. The motion passed.

A bit about Maurice—he had received the Legion of Honor meda, France's highest honor. He was born in New York; his mother was French. The family moved back to France when Maurice was a child for a while and Maurice was fluent in the French language. During World War II he worked for the U.S. Office of Strategic Services with the French underground. (The Office of Strategic Services became the CIA after the war.)He had been honored by the League for Christians and Jews as "Man of the Year."

I was just a little old widow lady from Reno, Nevada. Nevertheless, declaring gemstone treatment as a seller was the right thing to do. Mainly it protects the seller from charges of fraud. It also informs the buyer. It took many more discussions and motions to set the standards for the gem industry to require treatment to be declared by the seller. Treatment declaration is now required by all AGTA dealers and most of the rest of the trade has followed this lead.

I'm not sure what I did to annoy Zajicek, but as time wore on, tensions grew. Before and after meetings I began to have nightmares. Assassination dreams — in one dream I was riding in the back of a black limousine sitting between two men (I don't think they were other board members). Another car came racing past and someone in the other car fired a gunshot; the guy next to me died. I woke up in a sweat. In another nightmare I was crossing the Brooklyn Bridge and thugs came from both directions carrying chains and knives with the intent to kill me. Again I woke myself up in a sweat. I had gone to New York several times to do the New York Jewelry Show, but I'm not sure I ever saw the Brooklyn Bridge in person, much less ever walked across it. Obviously, this indicated that serving on the board was creating stress. Three meetings a year were held. One was held after the Tucson show since all the board members were already there. Then there was a meeting later in the spring and one in the fall. My first year, the meetings were in Phoenix. The second year when Zajicek became president the meetings were held in Dallas. It was a lot of flying, a lot of stress. The positive side for me was that I learned more about how power structures in the world work. I learned about my insecurities and realized they are a challenge for everyone else. I didn't "enjoy" the experience, but being on the board was one of the most important parts of my life. The dinners and cocktail hours were the fun part, unless someone carried a grudge after the meetings.

Some of the East Coast dealers on the board finagled space for AGTA members to participate in the New York Jewelry Show held in mid-July. Then the show was held in the ballrooms of the Hilton and the Sheraton at mid-town. As a board member I decided to participate, since board meetings were then scheduled after the show. Space allotted to AGTA was on the eleventh floor of the Sheraton located on Sixth Avenue. Of course, at a big jewelry show being placed in a very obscure location out of the ballrooms did not bring in a whole lot of business. A couple of years later the whole show moved to the Javits Center and AGTA had space that attached to all the rest of the show dealers.

After the show moved to Javits, Cheryl Kremkow left Hong Kong and was now in New York. This supreme jewelry journalist invited me to stay at her place. Going to New York has its perks. Oddly, the only restaurant that stands out in my mind was a little café with counters on Fifth Avenue that served divine blintzes. (I never could find a good blintz in Reno, not even a bad one.) When the board met we would go out in a group. The food was always good, but not memorable. Perhaps the cocktail hours clouded my memories. Dinners with the "boys" are quite dim in my mind. Boring? Maybe. There was nothing glamorous about all this travel — work days were long and sometimes tedious. There were few stolen moments for sight-seeing.

What little spare time I had in New York was spent at Saks Fifth Avenue. Their big summer sale was going on in mid-July. And they had a less expensive line of career clothes on the fifth floor that I could afford. They had a good selection of washable silk clothing which I found to be the most practical to travel with. Silk is light weight and feels luxurious to wear. I would unpack my suitcase and hang the silks in the bathroom, turn on a hot, steamy shower and all wrinkles would disappear. Hong Kong was another great place to buy washable silks, especially at the numerous clothing outlets that lined the streets.

Best of all, in New York, is the Metropolitan Museum of Art. Over the years I went to New York, I visited the Met as many times as I could. It was always hard to leave the Egyptian section with the Temple of Dendur. Eventually I would drift upstairs to marvel at Impressionist paintings. An art "fix" always felt healing after a lot of flying.

I racked up a bunch of air miles. I figure during my three years on the board I was flying about 50,000 miles a year. One year I was flying home after the New York Jewelry Show. I had to change planes in Dallas. Weather delays in Dallas were fairly common. My flight delayed about one hour. We boarded the plane about 6:00 p.m. The plane started down the runway and I had a horrible sense of panic. Normally I'm not a nervous flyer, but this time I had a feeling about "crash." I couldn't explain it, it was horribly scary. When the plane lifted off the runway the fear subsided. The next evening my parents were at my house for dinner. My dad turned on the evening news. That day there had been a crash of a Delta plane in Dallas around 6 p.m. Extreme wind shear caused the accident. I had been in that air space exactly twenty-four hours earlier. My first premonition—I didn't know that's what it was when we took off.

The creation of AGTA had been a success, so super-organizer Roland Naftule enlisted dealers around the world to create the International Colored Stone Association (ICA). The first meeting was planned for May, 1985. AGTA board members were expected to join and attend the first meeting in Idar-Oberstein. I made my reservations for the trip and booked a flight for Paris.

Good news came late in 1985: Apichart and Lenard negotiated their way back to Bangkok. The interest rate stabilized to a lower rate. Apichart made deals to pay off his creditors. This made my life easier.

- Lesson eighteen: If it is harmony you seek in life, stay out of political situations.

## Chapter 11 - AND THEN THERE WAS PARIS

May 13, 1985--Paris, France

Paris! I had never been there. It seemed to be a logical stop for a few days on my way to Idar-Oberstein. The dollar was strong at this time so I booked three nights at the Ritz Hotel and three more nights at a much cheaper hotel that was around the corner from the Ritz. I taxied from the airport and got a giddy feeling as we turned into the Place de la Concorde. Three days of staying at the legendary Ritz! I checked in to this very formal and sophisticated hotel even though I am neither formal nor sophisticated. My room was an upper floor garret with windows tilted upward towards the sky. If I stood on a chair I could see the famous Luxor Obelisk. I'm sure it was one of the Ritz's bargain rooms with an "almost" view. First thing I showered, changed clothes, and left to see the famous sites. As soon as I left the room, someone came in, put clean towels on the heated towel bars, straightened out my carelessly unarranged shoes and made certain my clothes were properly hung. This drove me nuts! I wasn't raised with maid service and I never cared if my shoes were lined up. But the neighborhood is cool — Chanel's shop is nearby as are many more designer shops. The reality was I couldn't afford "designer." Most of my wardrobe consisted of Macy's sale items.

Boulevard, a French word, clearly sets the standard for the ideal street. The Champs-Elysees, wide and straight, seems like the perfect parade route. Yet the buildings lining the street maintain a gray conservatism. Quiet storefronts with somber exteriors mask the flamboyance hidden inside. Arches and obelisks remind one of the power of the short reign of Napoleon. Just walking around, it is obvious why Paris has dominated fashion and elegant living. It's not cheap and gaudy like Las Vegas, just the opposite. The lure to take one's cash lies in lust for personal decoration. I finally found a shop with beautiful things I could afford and bought a pale yellow suit.

The first day I went to the Louvre. The museum is overpowering and cannot be viewed in a short time. For me the Louvre had too much Renaissance art to take in on one tour. I hunted down the "Mona Lisa" and was disappointed at its small size compared to the immense "Rape of the Sabine Women" that hung on the adjacent wall. How could a portrait of a homely woman compete with the action and chaos of the Sabine women? On my walk through the museum, I found some cases showing historical "gems." It was apparent to me that these "gems" were glass replicas. (I do have a trained eye.) One hopes the real gems are stored in a secure place. Regretfully I was too overwhelmed to look at the ancient art--Egyptian, Hittite, and so forth. I'll have to go back to check these sections out later. The Louvre is like a long freeway with no off ramps so you have to walk through the whole place to exit.

The Orangerie, which had Impressionist art, was close to the Louvre at this time. These paintings were the exciting ones for me and there weren't so many that it was overwhelming. Most of these Impressionist works were later moved to the Musee d'Orsay. The next day I toured the Centre Pompidou to see the modern art. The Pompidou is a multistoried modern building and it is easier to see one floor of art, digest it, go to another floor, digest that, and so on. It's easier to escape from than the Louvre.

I hadn't realized how far north Paris is located. In May the days are very long. Darkness didn't set in until 10 p.m. For me this was an opportunity to walk around later in the evening. What was wrong with this idea? Single women walking around in the evening were apparently assumed to be prostitutes. Since I was in my mid-forties I had no doubt that I could take care of myself and I never thought that I could look like a streetwalker. Then, maybe, I don't know how these women of the night look. One evening while I was still staying at the Ritz, a guy followed me, speaking in French. I kept walking faster and faster mumbling "I don't speak French." As I approached the front of the Ritz, he peeled off. The next night I decided to stay in my room. How many nights had I spent with Robert Ludlum and the eternal quest for Carlos the Jackal? I saved Ludlum books for long trips, great reading on a plane when the chase would go on for fifty pages without food or sleep for the hero. Since this was my first luxury hotel experience I wasn't prepared for the 8 p.m. phone call from the hotel staff. A voice said, "Will there be anything else, Madame?" "No, thank you!" Did the hotel staff have some sort of spy system? They seemed to know when I was in my room and when I left. This seemed kind of creepy. Again I found staying in my room during the last few hours of daylight seemed stifling and boring. I was happier at the cheap place around the corner.

One evening I looked for restaurants that appeared to be filled by locals. I ended up at the Hippopotamus. It was a large open noisy place with a simple menu. Steak and fries — the real French food, accompanied by a salad and a glass of red wine. On some level I liked going to Europe in order to eat the "pomme frites." Here fancy sauces were conspicuous by their absence. Of course, when in France one must take advantage of the set menu lunches and pastry shops.

While I was still at the Ritz, I got a phone call from Maurice Shire (yes, that "people like you" Maurice Shire). I had no idea how he knew my whereabouts. The AGTA board members must have had some secret spies. Was I becoming paranoid? He invited me to dinner. Maurice knew the good places since he had spent many years in France. We went to a restaurant across from the Opera. He told me that Sarah Bernhardt had sat where I was sitting. He was extraordinarily polite. I looked at the menu and it was beyond my French cognition level and I asked him to order for me. The first course was extremely rare liver with a delicious sauce followed by a very rare beef entrée. Not my usual fare, but when in France.... It was a lovely evening and I didn't detect any animosity about the treatment issue response at the earlier board meeting.

The best way to know a city is to walk everywhere. I've been lost about twice in my life, once in Paris. Early one morning I went out for a run and was lost in thought and ended up just plain lost. Paris was designed in a circular manner that follows the river. (I could never get lost in Manhattan set up with a Roman grid pattern.) I kept running until I reached the Arc de Triomphe and then I knew where I was. Shopping in Paris is fun if you happen to find the places you can afford. I found a second-hand dress shop which suited my budget. In the evening I continued my stroll, regardless of those guys looking for prostitutes. The weather was perfect and I had a lot to see.

My last night in Paris I decided to walk up to Montmarte, the hill that overlooks the city. Montmarte has to be one of the most interesting sites of Paris with its art studios and night clubs. It is crowned by the white domed Basilica of the Sacre Coeur which has been inspiration to many artists. I had a couple of hours until dark and was standing on a corner waiting for a stop light. Some guy spoke to me in French. "I don't speak French." I said in my standard reply.

"I speak English," he stated. "Where are you going?"

"Montmarte."

"I'll walk with you." That was a statement.

He seemed pleasant enough, medium in height, thirty-ish, clean and neat, well-spoken and rather ordinary. There was no way I could keep him from walking to Montmarte. We started a conversation. I hadn't talked to anyone except for Maurice in almost a week. I guess I felt a bit lonesome. After a couple of blocks, he said, "Turn down this way." Okay, I know my directions and that was not going to Montmarte. Now my curiosity got the best of me. We walked a couple of blocks and he steered me into a Middle Eastern restaurant. He ordered appetizers and seemed like a decent guy, intelligent, with a good sense of humor. I still felt confident I was in total control and could take care of myself in any situation. I told him I was leaving Paris the next morning, headed for Reims, then going on to Germany after a day in Reims. How could one go to France and not visit the champagne capital? After the appetizers we walked a few more blocks. He told me he was from Syria and spoke four languages and was looking for an engineering job. Obviously I was not going to Montmarte that night. Montmarte? I returned to Paris three more times over the years, and I have never made it to Montmarte.

It was getting dark. He next guided me into a bar. The clientele in the bar looked a little sleazy, so I asked to leave and he walked me back to my hotel. He said good night and asked if he could join me for coffee in the morning. I said "okay." I was leaving and I knew I was safe. Or was I?

The next morning he showed up promptly at the agreed time. We talked over dark and delicious French coffee and croissants. I was ready to go to the train. We stepped outside and I hailed a cab for the Gare de l'Est. Then he hopped into the taxi and said, "I'll ride to the station with you." Okay, no big deal. At the station I bought my ticket. Then he bought a ticket. Now I began to get worried.

I glared at him and snarled, "You are not going with me! " When does "no" mean "no?"

"You can't stop me! " he replied.

I finally realized I had a problem. I never even imagined his actions. Thinking I was in big trouble, I boarded the train. I was not a pleasant traveling companion at that point.

"I don't have a visa for Germany, " he confided.

"Fine, I'll just go on to Saarbrucken," I announced confidently. Saarbrucken was just over the French border in Germany and was on my route to Idar-Oberstein. I had found my escape plan.

At this point we came to an agreement. He would go with me to Reims and return to Paris in the afternoon. If he didn't board the returning train, I would catch the next train to Saarbrucken. Fortunately there were many trains running back and forth between Reims and Saarbrucken.

We arrived in Reims. I found a cheap hotel close to the train station and I left my suitcase at the front desk. I was afraid to even go to the room. If I needed to leave early I could grab my bag and go on to Saarbrucken. Unfortunately my running shoes were in my suitcase.

Reims is the center of the champagne industry in France. Around the time of Charlemagne, literature and religion were centered in Reims. Reims Cathedral is one of the famous tall Gothic cathedrals in France. Originally built during the 13th century, it was destroyed by fire and rebuilt in the 1400s. It was destroyed again in World War II and rebuilt again. It's filled with magnificent religious sculptures and stunning stained glass windows. Flying buttress architecture makes it a tourist attraction. What I found most interesting were the gargoyles placed around the edge of the roof. We walked around the cathedral studying the gargoyles — protectors of the church, keeping it safe from the outside evil. Where was my protector?

After coffee and a light lunch the stalker and I bought a chilled bottle of Tattinger's. We went to a park and uncorked the champagne and drank from paper cups. I was pretty sure he was leaving on the train back to Paris soon, so I could relax. What he was really looking for was an easy "green card." No, I wasn't going to be a party to that. He had a funny sense of humor and we sat there and laughed and drank champagne until it was time for his train. Thankfully, he actually boarded the train back to Paris. I breathed a sigh of relief and went and bought two more bottles of champagne for future use in Germany. Then I walked around the cathedral talking to all the gargoyles. I think they had a lesson for me. I'm not sure what that lesson was.

May 20, 1985-- Idar-Oberstein

The next morning I boarded the train to Saarbrucken with my extra champagne. At Saarbrucken I changed trains for Idar-Oberstein. I had the routing down at this point. BettyAnne had helped me at the Tucson shows and had become acquainted with many of the dealers. She joined ICA and we planned to meet at the Sonnehof Hotel. I liked the location of the Sonnehof in Veitrodt, a small village about three miles from Idar-Oberstein proper. It has newer homes and country-like solitude.

After I unpacked my bags, I needed some time to unwind from the little French adventure, so I walked down to the nearby section of the Black Forest. I had spent all my mountain hiking time in the California Sierras with tall conifers of pine, fir, and cedar. In the Schwartzwald were small fir trees with tiny trunks grown together into a nearly impenetrable mass. Nevertheless I stepped into the crowded woods. Little light made it to the floor of the forest. (I guess that is why they called it the "Black Forest.") I lost my sense of direction since I couldn't see beyond the space that I was standing in. I started to laugh. What if I never found my way out of there? But these sections of forest were quite small and it was unlikely I would never find my way out. I guess this was some kind of personal test or maybe I was totally crazy. After about forty-five minutes I wandered out of the forest onto the road into Veitrodt and walked back to the Sonnehof.

BettyAnne and I had our room on the third floor. I was walking down the stairs to go for a swim (swimsuit on) to cool off from the forest adventure. An AGTA board member, Richard Krementz, was coming up the stairs with his employees. One I had already met, the other was French by birth. Richard introduced us and the French-American, Guy, took my hand and kissed it. Rumor had it that he was the best buyer in the business.

A cocktail party started off the ICA Congress. About sixty members attended the Congress — all men but for BettyAnne and me. Wives were apparently left home for these occasions. By now I knew this was a man's occupation and world. A bus came to the Sonnehof to pick up the ICA participants and we went to town for the cocktail party held at the Meridian. The assembled group included Germans, Americans, Israelis, Sri Lankans, Thais, Africans, Swiss, French, Brazilians, and Indians.

This was the first Congress and for me the most fun. This Congress lacked the evening's entertainment of the later Congresses which were held in large hotels that housed all the activities. In Idar, the Meridian was "meeting central" during the day and the evening parties were held in more exotic locations.

Frankly, I'm not good cocktail party material. Small talk is very hard for me. The truth is I'm wallflower material. I don't walk up to strange men and begin the conversation. What do you say to a foreign dealer, "What is your stone specialty? Miner? Cutter?" Betty Anne was more comfortable with this gig. The men seemed to huddle together, talking about their mines and the cutting business.

The next day the real meetings began. I was there, but I can remember nothing of the meeting. But the first evening festivities were held at a medieval castle in the region. Ancient stone castles line the rivers of Germany. Like many ancient communities they were built on the high point in the neighborhood in order to see a possible enemy coming in for an assault. Everything in the castle was a gray stone, the most available local material. The next evening the party was on a boat restaurant on the Moselle River. A Thai dealer with a long Thai name who adopted "Mr. Very Sexy" as his moniker for the meeting, led the evening sing-along. The group was getting acquainted and all the partyers were in attendance. The last night was supposed to be a black tie affair. I hadn't read the schedule before I left home and had not brought formal wear. I managed to fake it with a red silk outfit and nobody cared anyway. By now everyone was comfortable together and the party actually started on the bus to the party location. One more bottle of French champagne gave its bubbly pleasure. This last party was at an ancient monastery that had been converted to a banquet hall. Candle lighting created a beautiful romantic atmosphere. The different evening venues made this Congress very special.

This first Congress gave me an opportunity to see the gem business in a wider perspective. It is truly an international business and the Congress created opportunities for the various players to meet and widen their business contacts.

- Lesson nineteen: Attention control freaks: you can control yourself. You cannot predict or control the actions of others. Watch out for the men on the streets of Paris.

## Chapter 12 - ICA #2

May 14, 1987--Bangkok, Thailand

ICA held its second Congress in Bangkok, "party central."A new luxury hotel, the Shangri-la, had been built on the banks of the Chao Phraya River offering plenty of conference space and an exquisite location just off New Road. This time I had my party clothes and was ready to rumble. I arrived at the hotel around midnight, checked into my room, fell asleep for a few minutes and woke up around 2:00 a.m. I envy those people who can fall asleep easily, sleep anywhere, especially on planes. Fortunately I can stay awake a long time. Wide awake, I dressed for a run through the streets. I ran into Krementz and Guy on my way out of the hotel. They looked at me as though I was crazy. Regardless of that apparent truth, I ran up Suriwong Road to Patpong Road. There were plenty of people on the streets, but the action on Patpong was apparently over. Patpong Road houses the sleazy night club acts that, in my opinion, tarnish Bangkok's reputation. After the run I finally fell asleep for a few hours. As crazy as that might sound I felt very safe in Bangkok. People on the streets might laugh and point at a woman running alone, but it is good-natured.

The number of attendees had increased substantially since the Congress in Germany. "Mr. Very Sexy" had enlisted many new Thai members and they were going to put on a spectacular conference. As people from all over the world arrived for the first day, most of us hung out in the bar. Mid-afternoon Ray Zajicek (the emerald dealer) was having a discussion with Campbell Bridges (tsavorite garnet miner). They were arguing about which was the better green stone — emerald or tsavorite. As each portion of vodka was consumed, the discussion got louder. Drinks were being chugged, not sipped. There would be no winners in this skirmish, and as hysterically funny as this mini-war was, the participants were fighting in all sincerity. The battle became intense and finally they stood up and it appeared they were heading outside for a scuffle. (I can't believe how adult males act sometimes.) Cooler heads intervened and the two parted. This conference promised to have some lively action.

Campbell Bridges was a legend in his own time — a Scottish geologist who had settled in Kenya. He discovered an intense green transparent form of grossular garnet in the Tsavo National Park. When he introduced the stone to Tiffany & Company, they marketed the stone as "tsavorite." Tsavorites are found in a range of light to dark green tones. They are slightly more yellowish than emerald. A few could pass for emeralds. Tsavorites are only found in this one location in Africa; they are much more rare than emeralds. Bridges was legendary for fighting off attacks from lions and surviving in a wild environment. On my flight back home Bridges sat across the aisle from me. We talked about gems, of course. Tragically he and his son were hacked to death in 2009 by men who blocked the roadway to the tsavorite mine. When they got out to clear the road, a gang armed with machetes attacked and killed them. This horrible death shocked gem dealers around the world. It was a news item on NPR (where I heard it).

The Congress began with a promotional film featuring colored stones as romantic gifts that men give to women. Obviously it was influenced by diamond marketing strategies. I watched this film in shock and got angry. It was the 1980s — Margaret Thatcher was Prime Minister of Great Britain; Sandra Day O'Connor was a Justice on the

Supreme Court, and Geraldine Ferraro was a vice presidential candidate. Hey, guys, wake up! Many women had hung up their aprons and were out buying their own jewelry. My experience told me while men will buy women diamonds, it is women who will buy colored stones. I thought the ICA had blown a lot of money without doing market research. The guy sitting next to me said, "Sitting next to you is like being next to a volcano." True! When the film was over I went up to the stage and took the microphone and slightly incoherently raged on that these boys did not know who the market for their product was or what the influences of the market were. In their defense, these were miners, cutters, and wholesale dealers who did not sell their stones on the retail market. I knew that the market for colored stones was women. Colored gemstones offer more affordable beauty than diamonds and are more easily designed into everyday wearable pieces. Fashion dictates what colors are popular from one season to another.

I did a good job of pissing off everyone. No, I hadn't been tactful. I just reacted and said what I thought. When the break for lunch came there was a bunch of tall Germans waiting for me at the exit. By then I realized my response was pretty offensive and I was a bit frightened by them. I had borrowed jewelry that I designed from one of my clients. (I made jewelry to sell, I couldn't afford to keep it.) I was wearing a large bluish green tourmaline pendant with a princess cut diamond crown. The Germans wanted to look at the piece, after all it was a bit spectacular and I think they were impressed. Lunch was served and I sat alone; no one wanted to be seen talking to me. I began to worry, could these guys get rough? Was an assassination plot brewing? I kept quiet the rest of the conference. The second day a couple of dealers came up to me when no one else was looking and whispered, "We think you were right." Then they scurried off before any one saw them talking to me. By the third night I actually had people sitting around me at dinner. The humorous offshoot of this was that in the trade magazines a few months later, various men were quoted saying, "Fashion dictated the market for colored stones," and that women constituted a large portion of the market for "color stones." At least they were listening.

ICA gained a much wider membership since the Idar-Oberstein Congress. The big players were here and out of my league for business contacts.

Every evening at this Congress was a black tie extravaganza. One evening Thai women performed in their traditional dance. The next night an elephant was center stage with acrobats. The end of the Congress concluded with fireworks over the river. I can't remember the food, curiously.

- Lesson Twenty: If you express an opinion harshly, expect the fallout. And be sure you are accurate in your opinion. Try to sound coherent.

## Chapter 13 - ANTIQUITIES

Sometime, 1988--Reno

A couple walked into my office looking for an engagement ring without a diamond center stone. The woman was tall and slender and in her thirties. He was shorter and older. Both were English professors at the University of Nevada. Diana MacDonald and Husain Haddawy were getting married after a ten-year courtship. I showed them my stock of rings and they chose an emerald and diamond ring with a traditional design. They invited me to the wedding and reception which was set out with delicious Middle Eastern delicacies. The crowd included many of Husain's Iraqi family members and I peeked into a new culture.

A couple of weeks later Dr. Haddawy came in with some ancient Sasanian stamp seals. The Sasanians had taken over the rule of Persia in 226 A.D. They created a huge empire ranging from the Persian Gulf to the Caspian Sea and east into Afghanistan and to the borders of India. Zoroastrianism was the state religion. After the death of Mohammed in 632 A. D., Muslim armies invaded and destroyed the Sasanian Empire. Dr. Haddaway's seals were semi-circular polished pieces of agate with some figures engraved on a flat top surface. They were used as signature seals and were drilled with a hole in the center to be hung on a leather cord so they could be worn. The ancient owner of the seal thus had a functional item for signing documents and a personal amulet to protect and bring good fortune. This flashed me back to my favorite college classes, ancient art history, taught by Dr. Del Chiaro. Del Chiaro was an archeologist who had worked on Etruscan digs in Italy. He showed us slides of cylinder seals in class and at the time I thought cylinder seals were the most exciting things I had ever seen. Here, on my desk were ancient seals!   Husain wanted the seal cut so the flat carved portion was sawn off. These flat pieces were to be set in rings--I could arrange that. Then I bombarded him with questions. Where did he get the seals? He knew dealers in New York and London. I could sell these ancient pieces and I was going to the New York Jewelry Show.

Generously he made an appointment for me with an antiquities dealer.

July 1988 — New York

Habib Anavian had an office on Fifth Avenue. He ushered me in and gave me a book of his seal collection. Then he showed me an assortment of seals for sale, stamp seals and cylinder seals. I handled my first cylinder seal. The 3,000-year-old chalcedony piece measured about 1 ¼ inches in length, half inch in diameter, and featured incised carving around the surface. Anavian produced a piece of putty and rolled the seal across the soft surface, revealing a human figure flanked by two lions. I picked over the lot and found six I could afford. Here was my collection of ancient history in small stone carvings.

Seals evolved during the Bronze Age and were used in the Middle East, Mediterranean Europe, and North Africa (Egypt). Cylinder seals were the original security devices. Wet clay was applied around the edge of a jar or amphora on top of the leather lid. The seal was then rolled around the edge of the jar, marking the surface with its embossed carving. If the clay seal was broken it was evident that someone had tampered with the contents of the jar. A variety of gems and rocks provided strong, permanent material for the seals. Chalcedonies were readily available and frequently used. Especially beautiful were the ones made from banded agates and lapis lazuli. These materials were soft enough to carve and yet could take years of wear. Animals, men fighting animals and religious scenes were the predominant designs.

I visited the Metropolitan Museum while I was in New York and saw their cylinder seal collection in the Middle Eastern section. I thought of the possibilities I had now that reached back to my earlier interests long forgotten.

Meanwhile at home the Haddawys and I became friends. I would go to their house and Diana and Husain would prepare Middle Eastern cuisine. They would come to my house and I would cook soup, homemade hot baked bread and apple pie. These American dishes were Husain's favorites.

On their first visit to my house, Husain stated ironically, "My religion allows me to have two wives."I had to laugh at that (it was not a come on) and responded, "I don't think you could handle two wives at once."

The three of us shared many good dinners and I learned about Husain's background. He was born in Baghdad. His Sunni family owned property along the Tigris river and were well educated. He was progressive in his view of the world and attended western universities. Uncomfortable with the tight controlling culture of Iraq that conflicted with his liberal ideas of the world, Husain made his life in the West. Many Iraqi intellectuals moved away from repressive Iraqi regimes even before Saddam Hussein came to power.

For spring semester, 1989, Husain had a sabbatical in London. There he would be working with his Iraqi cronies. Together these expatriate Iraqi intellectuals were going to write the encyclopedia of the Arabic speaking peoples. They reserved an apartment on Queen's Way. On December 31, 1988, the Haddawys had moved out of their apartment, and spent a couple of days at my house before departing for London. I gave them a few days to get settled in London before I flew over. Husain had promised to take me around and introduce me to the London antiquity dealers.

January 6, 1989--London

After landing at Gatwick I took the train, then the subway to Husain and Diana's flat at Queens Way. The neighborhood housed many Arabs and exotic Middle Eastern restaurants. Unfortunately the apartment was not quite up to the Haddawy's expectation. Burn stains marred the hearth around the fireplace where prior tenants had open brazier fires, Bedouin style, in the apartment. Overall the place wasn't very clean. The kitchen stove was covered with grease and at night when you turned on the light, legions of cockroaches would emerge from their hiding places. Diana and I shrieked when we saw the roaches and then laughed about the absurdity. Cockroaches were not prevalent in Reno unless the area involved was super filthy. Husain and Diana needed to find a cleaner place when they became more settled. I'd been in some pretty bad environments in my travels, surely I could tolerate the roaches for a week.

On Saturday we went to the huge street fair on Portobello Road. This market has an endless variety of items, from antiques to vegetables. It was drizzling outside, but that didn't keep anyone away. Rain doesn't deter Brits, just those of us visitors from the Southwest United States. After wandering through booths with antiques, collectables, used clothing, and books, I found antique mother-of-pearl gaming chips. Betty Anne had been buying these in Tucson. Some jewelry designers were using these in unique jewelry pieces combining the old with the new. Late in the eighteenth century until the mid-nineteenth century these chips were carved in China and transported by clipper ships to England. These were the forerunner of Las Vegas-style gaming chips. Ranging from about one inch to two inches, the mother-of-pearl chips were carved into different shapes: round, square, rectangular, oval, and fish. Some were used for storing embroidery thread — these were square with notches for holding the thread. Older chips had relatively simple designs, scenes showing life in China or floral designs, or were carved into fish shapes. As time passed the chips became more ornate--some were heavily carved. Wealthy families had coats of arms engraved into the chips. Many of the better quality chips were personalized with initials. Jane Austen in her masterwork, *Pride and Prejudice*, mentions "winning fish" when Elizabeth Bennett attends overnight balls and card parties. You think they just danced all night? Read carefully and you will catch this. At the Portobello Road Market it was easy to find the fish and plainer, more ordinary pieces. The finer quality pieces weren't at the fair or someone got there earlier and bought them all.

Generally, I don't like big cities — too noisy, too much traffic, too crowded. But I love London, or to me, "Museum City." The best time to visit seems to be in the winter when the museums are less crowded. The British Museum is my most favorite place in the world. What's not to love: the Parthenon Frieze, panels from the ancient city of Ur, Egyptian and Greek sculpture, endless old treasures. The British plundered very well! Years later I spent a week in London and went to the British Museum every day, spending an hour or two each time. My head would get really saturated and I could take in just so much in one visit.

Other museums like the Royal Art Gallery, Royal Portrait Gallery, Victoria and Albert Museum, the Tate (both old and new) hold much fascination. The Victoria and

Albert Museum has a jewelry section, which I inspected with great interest. It appears that many of the gems are replicas, like the gems in the Louvre.

One time I went to London with my friend Nancy in January when tourists are scarce. We were at the Tower of London late one midweek afternoon and no one else was in the Crown Jewel Room. We were able to view the exhibit many times, over and over on the moving sidewalk that gives you a quick glance at the jewels. My impression is that the crown jewel display is the "real thing," not replicas.

Husain introduced me to his antiquity dealer friends who sold amulets and small ancient items. Besides cylinder and stamp seals, other gemmy pieces emerged. We found Persian signature seals with Arabic inscriptions engraved into orange sherbet-colored carnelian. The carnelian slices were set into silver bezels with an extended back portion to hold onto while dipping the carnelian portion in ink. Attached to the top of most was a ring so they could be worn around the neck. Kept close to the body, they were the equivalent of having a pen in one's pocket so you could sign things.

Egyptian items were the most exciting. Amulets and scarabs were constructed from a variety of materials: stone and faience (also called "composition"). For the record, the Egyptians "invented" glass; they used it for jewelry and amulets. Ancient Egyptian pieces portrayed the religious and spiritual life in Egypt based on their creation mythology. It would seem that Egyptian and Greek mythology is all about dysfunctional families. Many versions of Egyptian mythology exist, but they all begin with the gods, Geb and Nut, who gave birth to several children. Osiris was the first born, Horus the second, Set the third, and Isis the fourth. The oldest brother, Osiris, became a great pharaoh and married his sister, Isis. (Incest was the royal way in those days.) Sibling rivalry was rife with the ancients and Set, the jealous evil brother, waged war on Osiris and after many evil plots, Osiris lost the battle. In full fury Set cut Osiris up into fourteen pieces and spread these bits and parts all over the ancient world. An inconsolable Isis, after discovering this, searched the ancient world gathering up the pieces. Of course there had to be a hero: the good brother, Horus, battled Set to avenge the defeat and death of Osiris. A fierce battle ensued and Set plucked out Horus's left eye. As the battle continued Horus eventually reclaimed his eye and defeated Set. Then Horus offered his plucked-out eye to the reassembled bits and pieces of Osiris. The eye was so powerful that it brought Osiris back to life. Consequently the magic of the Eye of Horus symbolized the rebirth of Osiris and resurrection, and became a common motif in Egyptian art and jewelry. As a symbol of rebirth, Eye of Horus amulets were layered into mummy wrappings to guarantee resurrection in the afterlife.

The ancient Egyptian pantheon had hundreds of gods in their more than three-millennium existence. Those gods honored would change from time to time and some were redefined to please the beliefs of the particular dynasty in power. Cats represented by the goddess, Bastet, symbolized fertility. Many cat mummies have been found; there were special temples for cats. The jackal symbol, Anubis, was the chief embalmer and guardian of the underworld. At death one's heart was weighed by Maat, who signified truth and justice, symbolized by the feather. The heart would be placed on one side of the scale and the feather on the opposite side. Those light-hearted ones would have passage into the afterlife. Scarabs, alias dung beetles, laid their eggs in dung piles. To the ancient Egyptian observer, this appeared to be an endless cycle of life with endless numbers of beetles emerging from the dung. Scarabs and other Egyptian amulets were carved from many gem materials: lapis lazuli, carnelian, and other agates as well as glazed composition. The flat bottom of the scarab provided the perfect surface for engraving, thus scarabs evolved into signature seals. Much of the ancient Egyptian jewelry contained turquoise and carnelian, found locally. Lapis lazuli was not a local material and had an interesting journey to arrive in Egypt.

Lapis lazuli is a "rock" rather than a crystalline mineral like most other gem materials. It is made up from sodalite, pyrite and calcite. The source of this deep blue velvety stone was Afghanistan. The lapis lazuli mine there has been in operation for 6,000 years and is located at an elevation of over 16,000 feet. This raises some interesting questions. Long before Gore-Tex and polyester fleece, animal furs provided warm clothing for icy climates. It's always chilly at 16,000 feet and visitors inevitably experience symptoms of altitude sickness which include vomiting, diarrhea, loss of appetite, and sleeplessness. Of course, those who routinely live in high altitudes adjust more easily, but no one really lives that high. In most of the world the tree line ends at 10,000 to 12,000 feet. There may be water, but no natural living sources of food, animal or vegetable. So these ancient miners must have had to wrap themselves in their yak furs from head to toe, pack up stores of yak milk cheese and climb up to 16,000 feet carrying food and Chacolithic-age tools to hammer out chunks of lapis lazuli. After they filled their goat bladder bags full of rocks they would have a choice of traveling to the Persian Gulf and transporting these rocks by boat or going overland through Iran and other Middle Eastern desert countries to sell them in Egypt. Obviously this would be an extremely tough journey. One question: who was snooping around at 16,000 feet to discover the lapis and when?

Amulets and seals leave a permanent record of history. They tell us the spiritual beliefs held in ancient times. The durability of the materials used, most often in stone, also indicates the importance of these objects. They were difficult to produce with ancient technology and carved to last. This fact alone tells of their value. Discoveries of amulets and seals reveal the influence of international trade and travel that existed in the Bronze Age cultures during the third millennium B.C.E. Cylinder seals tell us a story, a very short one-act play. A stamp seal or scarab holds one signature or symbol. If you visit every archeology museum around the Mediterranean (I've tried, but have missed quite a few) you will find that the cylinder seal (developed in Mesopotamia) eventually was used in Egypt and scarabs from Egypt were adopted in the Middle East and Southern Europe. The borrowing of artistic forms proves the existence of international travel and trade in ancient times.

I found many wonderful ancient objects in London and knew they would be fun to display at the Tucson show which started the first week of February. While I was packing, Husain gave me an antique Koran to take home to one of his university friends in Reno. No problem? This was a short time after the bombing that crashed a plane in Lockerbie, Scotland. When I went through American Airline security they asked me, "Did anyone give you anything to carry aboard the plane?" "Yes, a friend gave me a Koran."Eyebrows went up and I was pulled into a more secure area for a thorough search. The Koran was at the bottom of the suitcase. It had beautiful hand-painted pages and was quite old. Nevertheless I got a thorough interrogation. I had been interrogated before. It's a simple process, the interrogators ask you the same question over and over to see if your story varies. Of course, if you are telling the truth your story will be the same.

On one of the trips with Liz, we flew back from Bangkok on Singapore Airlines which stops in Hawaii. The Hawaiians want to do immigration and customs their way. If you have commercial goods to declare, you must remain in Hawaii for twenty-four hours to clear customs and work with a customs broker. On this particular flight, my bags came off the carousel right away. I had turned in my stone purchases to the customs people. I told Liz I would go get the rental car while she waited for her baggage. I waved to her and started down the corridor to exit. Suddenly two big Hawaiian officials flanked me and ask me why I was signaling another person. "I was waving that I was going to get a rental car," was my answer. They demanded that I accompany them into a security room and the interrogation began.

"Why were you signaling to that other woman?"

"I wasn't signaling, I was waving that I was leaving to get the rental car."

"What were you doing in Bangkok?"

"I was buying gems which I already gave to the customs agent."

They went through my suitcase, then they began to go through my purse thoroughly. On the bottom of my purse was a wadded up candy wrapper. "What is this?" they asked suspiciously.

"I bought a candy bar in Hong Kong and there were no trash cans on the street, so I put the candy wrapper in my purse." Did they think I was the kind of woman who would litter foreign streets?

Then they brought in Liz and began the interrogation with her. "Why was that woman signaling to you?"

"What signal? She was going to go out and get the rental car." She answered.

Obviously our stories checked out since we were telling the truth. After an hour of this nonsense, the Hawaiians — Americans! — let us go.

- Lesson twenty-one: Avoid "strange" behavior, like waving, when you are leaving or entering a country. (What's strange about waving?)

- Lesson twenty-two: It's interesting that I could make important business contacts out of my 100-square- foot-office on the fifth floor of an obscure bank building in Reno, Nevada, by word-of-mouth.

- Lesson twenty-three: When bringing valuable antique books (like Korans) onto an airplane allow extra time to go through security.

## Chapter 14 - Sri Lanka

May 17, 1989--Colombo, Sri Lanka, ICA Congress #3

The third ICA conference was to be held in Colombo, Sri Lanka. Ray Zajicek asked me to help on a fundraiser auction. The big decision: how to get to Sri Lanka from Reno, do I fly east or west? From the west coast, Sri Lanka is about equidistant going either way. After checking with all the possible flight sources, I found flying east would take about forty hours, one hour less than flying west. In spite of some less-than-pleasant experiences on international flights I'm not a nervous flyer, just a poor sleeper, so this did not sound fun. I chose the eastern route to save that one hour, and I embarked on what seemed to be an endless journey. Normally I travel as light as possible, but for these events I needed a large suitcase with work and formal attire, a different pair of shoes for each outfit and jewelry--now expected for an ICA Congress. Once the conference started there was a formal event every night, with the usual feasts, spectacular entertainment (with elephants) and socializing.

The first stop was a short plane transfer in London where I boarded Air Lanka. This short layover didn't even allow for shopping time at the fabulous shops housed at Heathrow Airport. Next was a three-hour layover in Abu Dhabi, United Arab Emirates. Seeing the airport in Abu Dhabi was almost worth the trip. The exterior of the airport consisted of an outer shell of pierced work filigree to allow light in, while still blocking out most of the intense Arabian sunlight. Polished stone faced the interior, resembling a Venetian palace. The Arab men were dressed in floor-length white shirts covered by finely woven sheer wool long vests trimmed with a gold binding. The women wore tunics over tapered ankle-length pants made from colorful silks. Middle Eastern opulence in this magnificent setting was like waking up in a scene from Scheherazade. I missed the fancy designer shops in London--no fancy shopping here! In spite of all the elegance of the airport, the shopping area was limited to meager local products. Oil wealth of the Middle East may enrich a few and build impressive architecture, but there is a dark side.

In the transit lounge were hundreds of South Asians, Thais, Sri Lankans, Indians and others, flying in to serve as domestics and laborers. Most of these passengers were women. I had jokingly called Lenard a slave trader, since he had recruited Thais to work in the oil fields of Saudi Arabia. Now I saw the truth in my joke. With my own eyes I saw the sad, poor mass of humanity. On the positive side there was work for many poverty-stricken Asians. Less than positive, it is a form of indentured servitude. What would the wealthy do without low-cost servants to do the undesirable domestic work? Are there minimum wage laws, days off, reasonable living conditions? Or is this a modern form of slavery? The extremes of wealth and poverty have always bothered me, because it seems the wealthy profit from others' poverty. Where is there a sense of justice? If servants aren't paid enough to improve their economic situation, they are stuck in a situation where they remain dependent on their employer, without positive options. Is this a conscious or unconscious decision by the wealthy employer? On some level do societies "need" the poverty class? This is true of much of the world; maybe Scandinavia is the exception.

On my trip to Mexico with Steve in 1971 we spent a few days in San Miguel de Allende. While we were looking for a good location on a hilltop to photograph the town below, we came upon the local toilet facilities: piles of human feces left in the open air. No pits or holes or burial for the feces were apparent. Nice way to spread disease. It was also apparent that many poor Mexicans lived in lean-to shelters that were hidden by high masonry walls. We met Americans who lived there so they could enjoy the amenities of cheap help. I'm not against hiring domestic help, I'm sure it is functional in many ways. But what is the long term effect of this way of life that has existed since the beginning of civilizations? This system of paid "slavery" seems to be self-perpetuating. Are the poor able to eventually transcend their poverty? Or is there a bigger question of lack of education leaving the very poor without the tools to improve their economic life?

The Democratic Socialist Republic of Sri Lanka, formerly Ceylon, lies off the tip of India. Archeological evidence shows it was inhabited about 30,000 years ago with migrants from the Indian mainland. About 7,000 years ago the sea level rose and created the island of Sri Lanka. Now the shallow Gulf of Mannar separates the two countries. By the 1600s the European trader-invaders had found this tropical paradise filled with trees bearing cinnamon bark, fabulous gemstones and pearls from the Gulf of Mannar. The Dutch East India Company, an early of example of corporate greed, came in and set up shop and dominated the economic expansion of the island from 1658-1798. Next, Portuguese sailors invaded and worked with the native rulers to get rid of the Dutch. King Rajsinha II played the Portuguese against the Dutch. Spain and England invaded to plunder the country with their own imperialistic domination. By 1815 the English prevailed until they gave Sri Lanka its independence in 1948. Exploitation was the driver of exploration.

A few centuries before sailing ships figured out the world really was round, Marco Polo traveled to Sri Lanka. In 1294 he wrote, " The pearl-fishers take their vessel, great and small, and proceed into the gulf where they start from the beginning of April till the middle of May. They go first to a place called Bettelar and then go 60 miles into the gulf. Here they cast anchor and shift from their large vessels into smaller boats.... The merchants who go divide into various companies, and each must engage a number of men on wages, hiring them for April till the middle of May. Of all they produce they have to first pay the king, as his royalty, the tenth part. And they must also pay those men who charm the great fishes to prevent them from injuring the divers whilst engaged in seeking pearls under water, one twentieth of all that they take. These fish charmers are termed Abraiaman; and their charms hold good for a day only, for at night they dissolve the charm so the fishes can work mischief at their will. These Abraiaman know how to charm beasts and birds and everything living. When these men have got into small boats they jump into the water and dive to the bottom, which must be a depth of from 4 to 10 fathoms, where they remain as long as they are able."

The Dutch East India Company imported Gulf of Mannar pearls for the ruling class and wealthy women of Europe. Dutch Renaissance painters created portraits of very rich women wearing fabulous long white pearl drop earrings. In this period pearls were the most rare and valued gem materials.

Sri Lanka contains a vast supply of gem treasures. "Ceylon blue sapphires" are the most valued of its gem wealth. But fancy colored sapphires and pinkish rubies bring good prices. Padparadscha, a rare orangish pink sapphire, is mined here as well as cool colored spinels, blues and violets. Mysterious shimmering blue moonstones come from Sri Lankan mines.

The ICA Congress in 1989 was sponsored by the dealers of Sri Lanka. I arrived four days before the conference and taxied to the Colombo Hilton to be sequestered for the following ten days. I'm sure there were some beautiful sites in this country, but it was not in my plan to see them during this trip.

My plane had arrived during the day, so I was able to see the part of Sri Lanka from the airport to the Colombo Hilton. The Hilton, located on the rocky coast, faced the Indian Ocean. I didn't see any sandy beach, but this was no vacation. A few days after I arrived, all the local shops and businesses closed down for several days to celebrate Buddha's birthday. I always wake up at dawn; I eschew blackout curtains so I always know when it becomes light. I would get up, put on my running shoes and head for the streets before the crowds of people were out. I didn't know what to expect, I hadn't known it was primarily a Buddhist country. I expected dire poverty, but I didn't see any on my morning runs of about four miles. In this tiny radius around the Hilton, I found a clean and peaceful life.

This was the first auction and there were no established procedures or organization. Gemstones were shipped in from members all over the world but most of them were hand-carried in by the Sri Lankan members. After the stones were unpacked, each stone or set of stones needed to be logged in, numbered, weighed, examined by a gemologist, boxed, photographed and catalogued. Over one hundred items needed these procedures. My job was typist. My mother-in-law had told Steve if he never learned to type, he would not have to do it, and could find someone else to do the tedious work. The guys on the committee also were not type worthy. Is this sexist or was I fortunate I had a real skill? I was used to a typewriter, but this job had to be done on Cheryl Kremkow's laptop computer. For me, using a computer was a new experience. The complexity of the computer slowed my typing progress.

An auctioneer from Sotheby's conducted the live part of the auction. Supplementing all this was a committee of Sri Lankans, Ray Zajicek, Cheryl Kremkow, and me. Ray, who basically ran the whole thing, was a "night" person. I work best from dawn until lunch, then it's downhill the rest of the day. Closely working with the very fine and expensive gems was my reward for the job. The stones included some incredible sapphires, parures of various stones, emeralds, rubies, spinels, tourmalines, topazes, aquamarines and more. Most stones were very high quality-- the top end of the colored gemstone market. These stones were destined for the high-end jewelry market that exists somewhere in the world where I don't normally go. Since there was no grand plan on how to process these beauties, chaos ruled. All-nighters worked for some, not for me. The typing needed to be done after all the other procedures were done. To finish the catalogue in time for the auction meant typing through the night. Total stress!

The auction was held at the end of the conference. Like the prior Congresses the attendees came from all over the globe. Big bidders supported the auction; I watched. One of the items that stood out for me among the predominant red, blue, and green stones, was an intense orange sapphire weighing around ten carats. This stone had been questioned by many: was it treated in any way to give it the very unusual orange color? The technology for making this determination was not available in Colombo. I did buy some fine blue flash moonstones from one of the local dealers, which were more in my price range.

Early one morning the phone rang in my room. It was Sydney calling from home. Of course, as soon as I heard her voice I was asking panicky questions, "Is everything all right? What's going on?" (She didn't usually call me when I was abroad.) She had received an application from an Eastern college that took high school freshmen and sophomores. I don't know who sent the application, but I told her to go ahead and submit it. This was just an application, how could I mind? Little did I suspect the outcome.

An exciting first auction led to Auction #2 which would be held in Hawaii. I packed my bags and took a taxi to the airport, which concluded my very limited sightseeing of Sri Lanka.

****************************

- Lesson twenty-four: I should have booked an extra day to see a bit of the country.

## Chapter 15 - European Tour

Shortly after my return from Sri Lanka, Sydney flew off with her tenth-grade German Club for six weeks as an exchange student to Freiburg, Germany. A few weeks later a letter came to her from Simon's Rock College in Massachusetts. Having just finished her high school sophomore year, she had been accepted into this unique college environment that was set up for kids who need more challenge than they would normally get from high school. There would be no high school diploma, but after two years she would have an associate arts degree. I talked to my dad about the finances, as he had a little fund set aside for her.

We planned a short tour of Europe after the exchange. Sydney's oldest friend, Donna, and I were to fly to Frankfurt to meet her and then we would drive to the beaches around the Mediterranean. Donna was living in the Seattle area and I was to meet her in Chicago for our overseas flight to Frankfurt. I don't know what happened, but I missed Donna in the airport because her flight was late. I had to make a hard choice of whether to miss my overseas flight or to hunt her down in Chicago. I called her home to tell her mother. We made the decision that I would proceed to Frankfurt and I would meet Donna there for a later flight. I waited at the Frankfurt Airport where I have so often been more than easily entertained, until the next flight from Chicago landed. There was Donna! We went to rent a car and I was offered a Honda Civic. Great, I had a Honda at home, it seemed like a good choice. What I didn't know!

Sydney wasn't coming until the next day, so Donna and I found a small hotel near the Rhine River for the night. The weather was warm and sunny and we found a restaurant overlooking the river. We sat on a terrace with a view of a crumbling ancient castle built on the edge of the river. What we didn't notice was that our hotel was a few yards from railroad tracks. Trains passed by all night, shaking the room as they passed. Next time in Frankfurt, I'll make a note to find a room away from the railroad.

We met Sydney's group at the Frankfurt Airport. The rest of the students were flying home to Reno. My first message for Sydney was that she would be leaving for college in the fall. So for me this was the chance for quality time with her before she left for college. Our crazy tour was to begin. I would have liked to drive the back roads of France, but this trip was for the pleasure of the girls and they wanted to hit the beaches of the Mediterranean as soon as possible. We got in the little car and took the Autobahn. Driving at ridiculously fast speeds is required, not optional, on the Autobahn. I'd be driving a full-out 90 m.p.h. for that puny Honda and suddenly some hot Mercedes would be on my bumper. At high speeds the little car felt like it would fly off the road on the curves. It was scary and I had precious cargo, Donna and Sydney, and I prayed we wouldn't crash.

Around dark we were in Southern France and turned off into Vienne. We saw a small hotel and went in and one room was available. Fine, I thought. The room was on the fifth floor of a 500-year-old hotel. The furnishings in the room appeared to be about 100 years old, and with all the dust that had accumulated since then. We were tired and didn't care. First, the door handle to the room broke off. We weren't secure but who cared, it was unlikely that anyone would climb the rickety five flights of stairs thinking we might not have a locked door. The bathroom had several issues — the shower didn't work, the toilet flushed funny. Nevertheless we crawled into the dust-ridden beds and fell asleep. At sunrise I was awake and snuck out of the room leaving the two sleeping girls and walked through town. The Romans had settled there during their world conquest. I wandered through the ruins of a coliseum, and the requisite bath houses. I would have liked to spend the day there, but when I got back the girls were dressed, packed and ready for breakfast. We wandered downstairs laughing about our less-than- perfect accommodations. However, the French coffee and croissants were divine, I think the best I had ever had — at least it's the only breakfast I can remember in my European travels.

We continued on the Autobahn until we ran out of road at Toulon overlooking the Mediterranean Sea. We found a small bed and breakfast on a promontory overlooking the sea and checked in for four days. Our itinerary was not fixed, but we had plenty of options here. Before dinner we went to the terrace and I ordered Kir Royales (champagne with a splash of kir) for the three of us. The normally easy-going Sydney glared at me and reminded me that I had promised we would have champagne on this trip. "Oh, you ordered some fancy mineral water again," she whined. I laughed at her and said, "Just wait." The Kir Royales were served in tall flutes and we sipped and viewed the sea. There was no more whining.

One day we drove to Nice and walked around the yacht harbor eating French ice cream. The yachts housed the ultra-rich. Huge fresh flower arrangements adorned the rear decks and people were sitting around with champagne flutes. Maybe these yachts housed the people that buy the jewelry with all the expensive stones I had seen at the ICA auction in Sri Lanka. A view of le beau monde.

Another day we drove up a narrow winding road to Grasse. From there we could look down on the very green rolling hills of the quiet French countryside. Fragrance from fields of lavender and other heavily scented flowers filled the air. We enjoyed a little French lunch and visited the many perfume shops. Finally we discovered our favorite fragrance of the day and bought small bottles.

Paris was our next destination and this time we traveled the slower country roads. On the way we stopped in Aix-en-Provence. The French Impressionist painter Paul Cezanne was born there and the landscapes of the area inspired much of his work. We arrived midday on a warm July day and walked through shaded streets to an art fair. We found some arty souvenirs and had one more great French lunch.

Then we were on the road to Paris. That evening we stayed at the little cheap hotel around the corner from the Ritz where I had stayed in 1985. If you are in Paris for a couple of days how do you choose what to see? We walked to the Louvre and the girls marveled at the impressive façade. We made our choice to enter the Louvre through the modern glass pyramid to use the restroom--and then we left the building! The Louvre was too intimidating. The d'Orsay across the river was our museum of the day. Our art tour in the d'Orsay was perfect, filled with French Impressionist work we could relate to instead of the endless collection of Renaissance works in the Louvre. Pastry shops along the street lured us in for sweet snacks. We dined at the Hippopotamus for dinner for a taste of the real French food, steak and fries. The next day our museum of choice was the Pompidou with contemporary art. Somehow the mid-summer energy was not as dynamic as it was in May during my first visit. The girls weren't too excited about Paris and they were totally weary of visiting museums. It was hot, the streets seemed empty. Apparently the Parisians had gone to the beach, so after three days we headed for Reims. We walked around the great cathedral ogling the gargoyles. A concert was scheduled for the evening at the church and we bought tickets. There is something magical about these old cathedrals—it's like they were built to reverberate with music.

The last stop before going home was Idar-Oberstein. The girls entertained themselves while I visited Karl Egon Wild, one of my favorite gem dealers, to look at his latest stone selection. It was rainy when we were there, curtailing any thoughts of walking through the town.

On the flight home we said goodbye to Donna in Chicago. When we got home Sydney had two weeks to pack for college. I didn't know how traumatic this "empty nest" stuff was going to be. The school was located in Great Barrington, Massachusetts about five miles from the New York state line. The closest large airport was in Albany. But I felt I needed to go with her for the first trip since the school was located away from a major airport, so I booked us to LaGuardia for a couple of days in New York. Cheryl Kremkow, who had taken a job in New York, kindly let us stay with her. Like Paris, New York has too much to see in a few days. We bought the half-price tickets for "Black and Blue," a music and dancing review, and hit the Metropolitan Museum. We shopped at Macy's and then we taxied back to LaGuardia to rent a car to drive to Great Barrington. As a lifelong Westerner, I'm pretty baffled when driving on the East Coast. I get confused in all those trees. I had good maps and had planned to drive up through eastern New York, but the road sign for the off ramp we wanted was covered by tree branches. There didn't seem to be any way to turn around. We ended up in lost in Greenwich, Connecticut. I couldn't figure out how to get back on to the freeway where I missed the turn so we headed north on the back route to West Massachusetts.

After a few moments of frustration we found a little road in Connecticut and began to pass old historic buildings and homes with signs showing dates from America's early years. How fortunate I was to stumble onto this road packed with history — sometimes getting lost has its benefits!

Eventually we arrived in Great Barrington and drove to the school. The dorm would open the next day. We drove to Lenox, had lunch and walked around town. We were planning to drive back to Great Barrington about twenty miles away but got stuck in an endless stream of traffic. In this quiet little area, it seemed like an awful lot of cars, so I started to follow them out of curiosity and we ended up at Tanglewood, the summer music festival site. Wow, what a find. There was to be a concert, so we bought tickets and sat on the grass and listened to Beethoven for the evening. I'd been to the Hollywood Bowl many times when I lived in Los Angeles, where we took picnics and enjoyed people watching. For us it had always been paper plates at the Hollywood Bowl. But here at Tanglewood people brought their picnics with fancy silver candelabras, nice table cloths and china to eat from.

The next day Sydney moved into her dorm room and met her roommate. We went outside to where the new students were gathering and Sydney joined her new life. I tried to hold back the tears as I got in the car to drive back to LaGuardia. I think this was one of the most difficult moments in my life. She was only sixteen. When you raise your child to be independent, as I had with Sydney, you have to be prepared when she actually becomes independent.

- Lesson twenty-five: Sometimes following the crowd takes you to new and interesting places (Tanglewood).

## Chapter 16 - ICA Auction in Waikiki

May, 1991 - Honolulu, Hawaii

ICA chose the United States for its next Congress. The buzz among the members was the rest of the world wanted to go to Hawaii, so the meeting was held at the Sheraton on Waikiki Beach. This was familiar territory for me, as I had lived there for a year in the early '60s, where I suffered "island fever.""Get me off this rock!" Too much flawless weather is not a good thing for me. Waikiki had grown into a concrete jungle since I had left. Where there had been little beach houses, plumeria trees, orchids surrounding little properties, were now concrete and glass high-rise buildings. I was totally acquainted with that stretch of beach. I had tried to learn to surf there. With fairly gentle waves constantly rolling in, the non-serious surfers would sit on their boards waiting for just the right wave. The serious surfers were up the road at Makaha or on the other side of the island at Sunset Beach. Body surfers would be at Makapu where the surf breaks close to the beach. At Waikiki the surf breaks some distance from the beach, so if you are lucky enough to catch the wave you can get a long ride into the beach and then paddle out to catch another. I had spent several weeks waiting for that perfect wave. I lacked the upper body strength to catch most of them. Surf boards were very heavy at that time, so I had to depend on catching that one wave that would accommodate my lack of strength and pick up the heavy board and give me a wondrous ride. Finally the day came. The board responded to the wave's power, I was on the crest, finally I had caught a good one. Well, for about fifteen seconds. Another guy, (a U.S. Marine identifiable from his hair cut) was on my wave. He cut in on my left and I could see I was headed for a collision. A game of chicken ensued, one wave, two people, who's going to bail out? Enough of my surfer chick ambition.

The second ICA gem auction brought me back to Hawaii. After Sri Lanka I insisted there be some organization for the auction. Since we were the host country we had control of running it. It seemed pretty obvious that gems had to be handled in a certain order so we put together an assembly line; log in the stone with the accompanying paper work, have it tested to be sure it was what the paper work said it was, assign it a number for the auction catalogue, box it for display purposes, photograph it, type the catalogue. We had a great team: Bart Curren photographed the stones, Roy Albers and I worked together with the paper work, boxing and typing. All this initial work had to be done before the Congress started so that the members would have time to come in and examine the stones before they went up for auction. Once the members came, Roy and I remained in the auction room to pull out the stones for the members to view them. Too bad I missed all the mining reports and other activities that went on in the Congress meetings. (No regrets.)

As I remember it, meals at this Congress were buffet style. With so much entertainment in the immediate neighborhood, there was very little formal entertainment accompanying the dinners. With all the international people coming, the buffet offered Indian and Japanese cuisines, both vegetarian and carnivorous. I went for the Indian dishes and was thrilled we weren't sitting at a banquet-style dinner always waiting to be served. I passed on the entertainment. Maybe there were some hula and Tahitian dancers. I might have been doing auction work or merely bored with all the dancing I had seen previously in Hawaii. One night was very memorable, however. After dinner, and many rounds of drinks, the Israelis and the Germans gathered around a couple of the large banquet tables and sang. There are times and places where the world seems to be a united place. The singing went on for hours, and it seemed the whole world must be at peace.

The auction went well and ICA profited, raising money for gemstone promotion.

Fall, 1991--Reno, Nevada

The Tucson show had continued to grow with more and more foreign dealers setting up in new shows. I couldn't compete with those dealers that I bought stones from. The shows were getting more expensive, and it wasn't fun anymore. So I decided it was time to quit having a booth in Tucson. Fortunately Tim Roark, a dealer from Atlanta with an excellent variety of gemstone inventory, allowed me to work in his booth at the show for a few days so I could get a bit of the Tucson "fix." At home my aging parents increasingly needed my help. I decided to make a big change and open up a retail store in Reno. One of the local jewelers was handling repair work for my customers, so I asked him if he wanted to partner for a retail store. I had a good clientele and I wanted to move away from the gambling in downtown Reno. In the fall we opened up the store, the Ice Palace, in a small mall away from downtown. We specialized in custom-made designs. Lenard was handling my jewelry manufacturing in Bangkok. The jeweler partner could do custom work for our customers and I could continue to appraise jewelry. The first year went fairly well. I didn't miss the long international flights.

- Lesson twenty-six: Organization makes thing much easier.

## Chapter 17 - Israel

June 16, 1993-- Tel Aviv, Israel

Another auction! This one would be hosted by the Israelis. Israel didn't excite me as a travel destination — what could possibly be of interest in a place of continuing strife between Israelis and Palestinians? Nevertheless I booked an El Al flight out of JFK in New York. To fly on El Al you must arrive two hours in advance of the flight, so I left home a day before and spent the night near the airport. El Al has an excellent safety record. Their pre-boarding process requires an interrogation first. A young woman took me into a small office and for almost an hour she went through my luggage and had a lengthy discussion about my visit to Israel. Okay, I've been interrogated before, no problem.

I had no idea what to expect in Israel. I taxied to the Tel Aviv Hilton and was pleasantly surprised. The hotel, situated on a bluff, overlooked the Mediterranean. In sunny and cool weather, I had this one day to explore the new environment before the auction process began. I showered and left the hotel heading south along the beach with no destination in mind. I proceeded along the sidewalk passing outdoor cafes filled with happy peaceful people. I kept walking about two or three miles until I reached the port city of Jaffa. A large sign at the entrance to the city outlined a brief historical time lineof this small town. The 4,000 year period recited invasions of the "Who's Who" of world and biblical history. It was founded in the 18th century B.C.E. by the Canaanites and has operated as a port continuously since then. In Christian belief it was thought that the city was named after Noah's son, Yefet, after the great flood. And this was the city from which Jonah departed in his flight from God just before he met the whale. In Greek legend, Andromeda was chained to rocks that faced Jaffa's shore. Later the Roman Legions invaded Palestine through this port. Richard, the Lion-hearted led Crusaders into this port on their way to Jerusalem. Napoleon landed here in his bid for world conquest. Then the Ottomans occupied this area for a couple of centuries before General Allenby of Great Britain routed them out in 1917. The Brits had control of their "Palestine Mandate" until 1948 when Israel became a Jewish state. The Jews and the Arabs fought over the city until 1950, when Jaffa became united with Tel Aviv.

The inflow and outflow of history here created Western civilization. Suddenly I had fallen in love with Israel. Jaffa had grown into a hilltop of history. Every invading culture had built their monument of civilization at Jaffa, one civilization on top of the prior one, history in layers leaving a record to be investigated by the modern world. Archeological excavations left deep holes in the cityscape. Jewelry stores, cafes, and small shops for tourists sat on the top layer. For me, Jaffa was an irresistible draw. When I had a chance to escape the auction tedium, I would sneak out and walk to Jaffa. These stolen moments were usually in the evening and when I passed all the little cafes on the way to Jaffa I saw happy Israelis our enjoying the pre-summer beauty of the sunset with music playing and people singing.

Tel Aviv, a modern city, developed after the Exodus in 1948. Every day preceding the opening of the ICA Congress the auction committee met at Eli Eliezri's office. The office was in a high-rise building in Ramat Gan, the area where the diamond and gem businesses were located. Ramat Gan is a major diamond cutting center. A few colored stone dealers have offices there. I'm sure that tight security surrounded this area, but it was not conspicuous. Eli's office had a kosher kitchen. Cappuchinos greeted our arrival every morning. We worked until lunch. Lunch included a fresh pita bread filled with chicken, tahini, and fresh Israeli tomatoes, served with Turkish coffee. No dairy was served at lunch—strictly kosher. I could live like that!

Once the Congress began, the auction work proceeded in the basement of the Hilton. The days working here seemed long and grueling. The dinners at the Hilton were endless drawn-out affairs with poor service and at least a half hour went by between courses. After the salad course I would get up and leave, change out of my formal clothing and sneak out for an evening walk to Jaffa. One night on my return, it was quite dark, an Israeli woman bawled me out and told me how dangerous it was to walk there at night. For me that was no deterrent. The tours of Jaffa were like entering another world, an escape into another era. I'd walk around and peek into the archeological excavation areas and forget all the auction stress.

On Saturday, the Sabbath, there were no meetings, no work. The Sabbath in Israel was strictly observed. A trip to Jerusalem was planned and I hadn't read the instruction letter carefully. It instructed women to wear skirts that covered one's knees. I had a skirt that fell right above my knees; this was not an era of longer skirts! When I attended these Congresses I was thinking about the auction, not whether I had appropriate wear for visiting sacred places. Earlier that morning I had been typing the auction catalogue from 4 a. m. until the tour bus left at 8 a.m. I received a mild scolding about my inappropriate skirt, and off we were to Jerusalem. We drove away from the Mediterranean into an area where young trees had been planted. Reforestation areas were constantly being replaced with trees the Ottoman Empire occupation had used up for fuel.

As we approached the hilly city, I felt a sense of déjà vu. In my mind I could hear the trumpets of the Roman Centurions blasting as we marched into the city. I sensed I was transported back two thousand years and was enlisted in the world's most powerful army. Then the tour bus wound up the road to Jerusalem, parked and we got out for our tour of the old City. The Old City is a divided city: Jewish, Muslim, and Orthodox Christian. Our guide led us through the narrow streets of the Jewish section. There were a variety of shops along the way. Carefully, our guide avoided the Muslim sections. Finally we ended up at the Church of the Rock. We negotiated our way through the fourteen stations and when we reached the "rock" part, I had to remove my outer jacket so I could cover my knees. We then proceeded down to the Wailing Wall. The faithful were at the wall with their prayers and their slips of written prayers to be placed between the blocks of the wall. The wall is a massive rock structure sitting below the Islamic Blue Mosque. Here is some of the most disputed real estate of the planet. Unfortunately a visit to the area around the Blue Mosque wasn't in our guide's tour — it seemed that he pretended that the incredible structure did not even exist. We were reloaded on the bus and driven to Bethlehem, about three or four miles from Jerusalem. The Church of the Nativity was built over the site where legend has it that Jesus was born. Under the church is the sacred site, a tiny space with a low ceiling; one must be stooped over to view it. Although I was glad to have this opportunity to go on the guided tour, there was much to see that I missed. On our way out of town the bus stopped at a selected tourist shop. You know these tours are basically rigged to profit the guide, but the visit was too short.

Sunday in Israel is a work day, so we prepared for the viewing portion of the auction. This auction did not make a profit and interest began to wane.

- Lesson twenty-seven: Read any information about sacred places. Prepare to bring appropriate clothing.

## Chapter 18 - Tokyo Auction

June 13, 1995,--Tokyo, Japan

Tokyo was the site of this ICA Congress. I arrived six days beforehand to work on the auction. The Congress was held at a hotel in the Shinjuku area. It was the same old thing, with the Japanese in charge this time. The first evening the Japanese auction chairman held a dinner meeting. I put on a very professional simple black dress and we went to a restaurant where I only saw men's shoes on the rack when we entered. That should have told me we were in territory normally forbidden to women. Our table was in a private meeting room with woven floor mats and no chairs. How nice to dine at a very traditional Japanese place where we would sit on the floor. Unfortunately my dress was not designed for sitting on the floor; the hem hit my knees but it was a fitted sheath and just didn't want to conform to a modest look when sitting on the floor. This wasn't my first trip to Japan, but somehow I hadn't anticipated this. I squirmed through the dinner and tried to pay attention to the plan being presented. Again my major job was to type the catalogue and help other "volunteers" during the earlier stages of putting the auction together. I was working with all new people except for Bart Curren, the photographer. I really doubt if Sotheby's or Christie's put together their auctions in six days. It was a high-pressure job—I loved doing it.

My other trips to Japan were very short and I had spent little time exploring. On this trip the Japanese culture was clarified for me. Tokyo, one of the world's largest cities, is relatively quiet. Mass transit serves the population well. It's no Los Angeles with endless traffic jams and honking horns. Nor is it Bangkok where the noise and polluted air dominate the landscape. People in Tokyo are also quiet and polite, despite millions of people crowded into a small area.

My time to explore the city was before sunrise. I found the local Winchell's Donut shop a few blocks from the hotel, bought my coffee and then wandered the streets. I would see couples just coming home from their date night at 5 a.m. There were hotels that rented rooms by the hour in this neighborhood. I wandered down by the river and found Japan's homeless people, who apparently packed up camp very early in the morning. Later in the day there was no sign of anyone camping out by the river. During the day there were no signs of poverty, no beggars or panhandlers. Perhaps homelessness in Japan is one of those secrets that society wants to deny. One evening I went out late wandering again. In Japan the street crews bring out huge lamps to light the workers doing road repairs. Once more politeness prevails and streets get fixed when it isn't an inconvenience to anyone. After my early morning wanderings I would return to the hotel, shower and dress for a lovely breakfast with a whole selection of seaweed to choose from. One particular bright green variety was my favorite.

Since typing the catalogue for the auction is the last thing to be done I felt the pressure right before auction viewing begins. Once again at 4 a.m., I got up to finish the catalogue. The rooms where we worked on the auction were completely dark and I didn't know where to turn on the lights. I felt my way like a blind person through a couple of rooms to where the computer was; fortunately it was in a room with a window, but it was still dark outside. Street lights provided a little light and I could turn on the computer and get to work. At 6 a.m. the Japanese chairman came into the room to check on me. Didn't he believe that I was responsible enough to get my job done even though it meant getting up at 4 a.m.? He acted very surprised that I was in there typing. And he turned the lights on. In this pressure- cooker atmosphere, there was no one to proof my typing. I had to be very careful and be motivated in order to finish on time.

An English language newspaper was slipped under my door every morning. Coincidentally, this Congress fell on the fifty-year anniversary of the end of World War II. For the time I was there, articles focused on resolution for the sex slaves that the Japanese military abducted along their trail of conquest in Asia. Finally, apologies and reparations were in order. Reading this, I was struck by the contrast between the war and the mid-nineties. Killing, rape, and destruction had been the actions in the early 1940s. Politeness, consideration, and harmony were the rule in 1995. I guess this sex slave issue hit me hard because these victims of war were women exclusively. Of course, in any war rape is not unusual. It has been this way forever.

Although World War II had been over for fifty years, its effects remolded the world map. Since I was born in 1940, I lived through the war and have faint memories of how it affected my family. The United States was desperate for officers to take commanding roles. They recruited men with college educations and ran them through a three-month course and rewarded them with an officer's commission. My father, one of the "90-day wonders" joined the U.S.

Navy and boarded a mine sweeper that cruised in San Francisco Bay. My mother and I moved to San Francisco--I have dim memories of Golden Gate Park. At the war's end my father was stationed in Norfolk, Virginia so my mother and I drove cross country to Virginia. It was mid-summer and I vividly remember the mosquitoes and the officer's club. It seemed to me at age four-and-a-half that the war was celebrated with mint juleps and a lot of bridge games.

The gem business had been massively affected by this horrible war. What if Hans Stern and others had not been transported to Brazil? What if Fred Pough hadn't been sent to Brazil to search for tourmaline crystals? These things affected my participation in gem buying. If Burma hadn't been overrun by the Japanese, would the development of gem mining have taken a different path? Of course, many more dire catastrophes resulted from the war — death and destruction. Massive migrations of people created cultural shifts.

When will "civil" become the rule in civilization? When will the world embrace humane behavior? Or somewhere inside us, is there a need for violence towards those who are in a weaker position? Again I was reminded I never think about these issues at home.

Although interest in the auction was in decline, one more was scheduled for the next ICA meeting in Brazil.

- Lesson twenty-eight: When working in a business dominated by men, wear pantsuits.

## Chapter 19 - Kilimanjaro

1996

Sometime in late 1995, Vicki Lynch, friend and accountant, said, "I've been reading *Travels* by Michael Crichton. He climbed Mt. Kilimanjaro. I think we should do that." My response should have been, "Are you out of your mind? When do fifty-ish women start climbing serious mountains?" But I said, "Yeah, let's do that." Vicki found an organized tour to Kilimanjaro that was scheduled for the first week of the following October. We paid deposits for the tour and planned a training schedule. Reno is surrounded by hills, some rather steep. January first we started by hiking up the steep hillside behind Vicki's house. On my morning walks, before work, I filled a backpack with books and walked uphill in my neighborhood. If I walked two miles uphill from my house I would hit the tree line of the Sierra Nevada Mountains. That spring we started going up to Truckee, California for our Sunday breakfast and we'd hit Donner Pass at 7200 feet. Both sides of the highway have good steep hiking trails where the Pacific Crest Trail crosses Interstate 80 a few miles above Truckee. For the Fourth of July Vicki borrowed a little camper and we drove to Great Basin National Park in Eastern Nevada. Wheeler Peak sits within the park with an elevation of 13,080 feet. We drove to the park on July third and parked the camper in a parking lot at 10,000 feet. That gave us about twelve hours to adjust to the higher altitude. The Sierra Club ranks this trail as "difficult." Starting out we were already in the climate zone where bristlecone pines thrive and the tall ponderosa pines were below us. For the first 1500 feet of elevation the trail wound through the bristlecones and a dense ground cover. By 12,000 feet, it was all rock to the summit. I was in better condition than Vicki and we agreed to climb the mountain at our own pace. By the time we hit the rocky portion I was ahead of her. Since it was the Fourth of July many others were on the trail. None of them were in their fifties, as Vicki and I were. Vicki, with gray hair, got many compliments on the way up. "It's nice to see you old people up here."

At these high altitudes it is never hot, so in spite of the brilliant Nevada sun, the temperature was pleasant. Above the tree line small rocks covered the mountain's surface and there was an obvious trail. The last 100 yards had large boulders with no apparent trail. I basically belly-crawled to the top, where there was a small flat spot, maybe 300 square feet. I just sat in the middle of that flat spot. Looking down from the summit is a 10,000 foot drop-off. I viewed mountains in Utah to the east and much of the mountainous areas of Nevada to the west. Other hikers reached the summit and told me that Vicki was on her way up. So I waited for her, trying not to dwell on how steep the drop-off was. About an hour later Vicki climbed up the boulders. She was thrilled to reach the top, but she had bone spurs in her feet and was in pain. Most of the other hikers had already hit the summit and were on their way down. Finally I demanded to take Vicki's backpack to lighten her load and we began the descent. Later she told me that she was in tears all the way back to the camper. I hadn't noticed. At that point she said she knew she wouldn't be in shape to attempt the trek to Kilimanjaro. I asked Sydney if she wanted to join me for this trek. Her response was, "I'm not that crazy."I had made a commitment to myself to go to Africa, so my training regimen continued.

Meanwhile the spring of 1996 brought some terrific losses. A very good friend of mine, Carol Page, died from lung cancer in March. Lenard died from AIDS in April. My father had a heart attack and died in June. My responsibilities to family became foremost. My stepmom needed care during the day. I was fortunate to find a nurse who would spend the day with her. I would go over there in the evening and fix dinner, walk the dog, and put her to bed. A few months later an old boyfriend of hers showed up and took some of my burden. He lived in Sacramento and would drive up for a couple weeks' visit. I could still maintain my training schedule in the morning. I needed the exercise to reduce my stress level. I had good employees, but running a retail business is never easy.

September 21, 1997--Nairobi, Kenya

I flew to London and boarded British Air to Nairobi. When I got off the plane my feet and legs were so swollen from edema I could hardly walk. I had five days before meeting the group for the trek. I spent one night in Nairobi before flying to the Masai Mara for a short visit in the bush. In Bangkok I had learned to drink tea to get rid of edema. After checking into my hotel I drank quarts of tea. The next day I had normal feet, so I taxied to the small airport that handled the short flights within Kenya. The Kilimanjaro climb had been the focus of my attention and I had given little thought to this side trip. A small plane landed, the passengers got out. One of the passengers had been air sick, creating a slight delay while the plane was cleaned up. Suddenly I burst into tears out of the sheer anticipation of this short adventure. All the stress of earlier events disappeared. The plane cruised at a low altitude and I could see the small encampments of the Masai. Forty-five minutes later we approached a dirt runway filled with a small herd of antelope, which quickly scattered into the bush. An endless vista of tall grassy areas spotted with small groves of trees stretched out before me. A Range Rover van from the camp that I had reserved was waiting for me. Animal migrations cross the Masai Mara after the rainy season when the fields of grass appear. Luckily I arrived at the height of the migration. A small river flowed through, providing habitat for the hippopotamuses. As we approached the camp, I saw giraffes, an assortment of antelopes, elephants and wildebeest.

The camp was very simple, almost primitive. The camp manager was a thirty-ish English woman. The rest of the staff were tall Masai men dressed in clean beige safari shirts with khaki colored Bermuda shorts. Secure individual tents contained comfortable beds for sleeping. The outhouse toilet facilities had a relatively fresh smell. The shower was a walled-in stall with a large water bucket was perched overhead. When you wanted a shower, you notified the staff to heat the bucket. When you were ready to rinse off you pulled a rope for a deluge of the warm water. This was a place of silence, solitude, and peace broken by quiet bird songs and occasionally a screeching elephant. A permanent building with a cement floor and metal siding housed a kitchen and dining facilities. I'm sure this was like the camp that Ernest Hemingway had when he wrote *The Snows of Kilimanjaro*. Bird photographs decorated the camp from the many bird watchers who had come as guests. Very fancy resorts existed in the area, but I was happy with Papa Hemingway's style. I was the only guest when I first arrived and I received great service. Simple but delicious food was prepared by an army-trained cook. Food was familiar: eggs and toast for breakfast, meat and potatoes for the other two meals. I'm sure this was a vestige from British occupation.

Every morning at 6 a.m. the Land Rover and driver departed for viewing the closest lion pride, which numbered nineteen members: the big daddy lion and about seven lioness consorts, and the rest were cubs. Big Daddy knew how to strut and he walked around the pride like the king that he was. The lionesses did the heavy work of bearing the cubs and running down the food supply. On my last morning on the Masai Mara we arrived to see the lionesses and cubs eating the remains of a large wildebeest. Suddenly Big Daddy showed up strutting his stuff. The females faced him, growling, and he retreated back into the bushes. About twenty minutes later he came out of the bush, his head lowered and tail dragging, as he crept in with a submissive posture. I couldn't believe I actually saw the extreme change in body language. In animals, body language is the surest form of communication. I had two cats at home, and should have noticed that before. At this point the females and cubs retreated and let him have what little was left on the skeleton. When the male cubs reach maturity they are cast out by the pride leader lion. These males live a lonely life as solitary creatures. We saw some of these outcasts hiding in the bushy areas.

One outing we drove to the small river to see the hippos. I was warned not to get too close. They are big animals and could be dangerous. Coexistence of humans and animals in Kenya is the rule.

For the first two days when we returned to camp, breakfast was served and we had time in the camp. In the late afternoon we would go out for another animal tour. Visitors are not allowed to wander off, for their own safety. I tried to leave the camp to go out for a walk, as I had to keep in condition. A young guard caught me and my escape was foiled. The next day a tall guide walked with me to a Masai village. We could see lion footprints along the trail. Neither of us was armed. He told me that if I left camp alone I could get lost. These guys worked to accommodate their guests. The Masai village consisted of low mud huts that had an outer waterproof dried mud coating. Flies swarmed, and the women attempted to be friendly, but they did not speak English. The men were out in the bush herding cattle. Herders stand on one leg armed with long sticks watching for predators. Not an easy life! When the area of their village is overgrazed, they move to greener areas and rebuild the mud huts.

One late afternoon we drove to a grassy area about a hundred feet from a small herd of grazing Thompson's gazelles. Hidden in the tall grass were two baby cheetahs. Mother cheetah assumed a low profile hiding in the grass awaiting an unsuspecting gazelle. Several Land Rovers gathered around including a BBC truck attempting to film the event. We were about a hundred feet from the mother cheetah. Sitting in the warm truck we were watching animals graze, while waiting for the cheetah to make her move. When there was no action, I struggled to stay awake. After an hour of waiting, one little gazelle wandered into the cheetah's territory and mama cheetah arose from the grass and began the chase. The gazelle responded quickly and bounded off towards the bush. With that gazelle's escape, lunch was lost for the cheetah babies. Mama retreated to her spot in the tall grass and resumed the wait. Again Mama saw a possible victim and again the gazelle was wary and took off. Another hour passed and more wary gazelles entered the area and avoided being lunch. I kept dozing off in spite of trying to carefully observe the cheetah. Finally one more gazelle entered the target area. Mama moved closer, moving down the grassy area in a low crouch. Suddenly she sprang into full speed and charged the gazelle. She was very close but the gazelle ran in a zigzag pattern and eluded the cheetah. Back and forth the chase and the charge continued. Finally Mama closed in and leapt onto the small gazelle. She opened her mouth and bit into her victim's neck. The gazelle went down with the cheetah on top. The cheetah waited until the gazelle was still, then she got up and went to her kittens and they followed her to a much needed lunch. We all cheered this kill in spite of the violent scene. The cheetahs don't make a kill every day. Big cats need to eat too. It would seem that an animal as fast as a cheetah would have little trouble making a kill. But the three-hour wait proved that it is not an easy process.

After the tour on the last morning, two young guides walked with me to a hilly area about five miles away. Armed with bows and arrows made from sticks and fine rope, we started the walk across the bush. One spoke English and I asked him, "Are you carrying poisoned arrows?" "No." I wasn't worried but I thought their weapons could hardly bring down a rabbit. We walked near a large herd of African buffalo. As we passed they went into motion. Large buffalo formed a circle facing outward with the calves standing in the middle of the protective circle. They watched us, carefully guarding their young. On the other side of the road was a large zebra herd. They just ignored us. When we reached the base of the hills we approached a uniformed warden, who protects the white rhinos from poachers. Five rhinos stood nearby, staring at the tourists. My impression that rhinos are vicious beasts that would charge people at any provocation was instantly dispelled. These docile beasts stood there while the tourists approached them up to five feet distance to take pictures. The Land Rover was waiting for us to return to camp. Near the camp was a large herd of elephants eating lunch of low hanging tree leaves. These creatures, too, were protecting their young. What kind of genetic connections do we have to the other species who value family as much as we do?

After lunch, I flew back to Nairobi to join the Kilimanjaro group. I had spent three nights on the Masai Mara with moments of extreme peace and solitude and hours of great excitement--I had totally forgotten all my domestic and business stress. These were the best and most exhilarating days of my life.

October 2, 1996--Nairobi to Tanzania

Ten climbers and two guides comprised our Kilimanjaro group. Three of us were women; the other two were with their husbands. Four of us were in our fifties, the rest were younger. The next day we would be bussed to Tanzania for the trek. We had lunch in Arusha, one of the centers where tanzanite rough is traded. No business for me on this trip! Back on the bus we drove through a desolate area at the base of Kilimanjaro that reminded me of Death Valley. A few ostriches were picking around the barren landscape in search of a meal. The bus took a left turn onto another road and within five minutes we were in a tropical forest. An amazing change! We drove a few miles to the entrance of the Kilimanjaro Park and the guides registered us for the climb. Four local porters were hired to carry all the gear, set up camp, and cook the meals. There are several trails to the top of Kilimanjaro. The guided tours take a route that takes one extra day in the ascent, giving the climber an advantage to acclimate to the extreme altitude. Individuals can come to the park and hire their own porters and go up the "tourist trail."

We spent the first night in a little rustic motel at the base of the mountain. Kilimanjaro is a giant mountain rising 19,440 feet out of a flat plain. Clouds surrounded the mountain when we drove in, but at dawn the first morning it was clear. Our porters were waiting for us. Each climber had his or her own backpack to carry extra clothing for temperature changes during the day, and a water bottle. Tropical forest with blue-faced monkeys lined the beginning portion of the trail. The guides instructed us to take rather small steps heading uphill and to pace ourselves. The trek took on a boot camp atmosphere of humorless hiking. This was not about exploration. We had a goal and the guides took their job of achieving the goal seriously. Up we marched in a long line, heads down looking where to place our feet, then stopping a couple of times for water, snacks, and finding a tree to hide behind for toilet activities. Each of us carried a bottle for water and purification tablets. We would fill up at each small mountain stream. The group moved at a steady pace the first day, leaving the tropical forest behind. The first day was easy, no altitude issues. Day two we climbed to 12,500 feet and camped at the base of a 1,000 foot basalt breach wall that was totally vertical—absolute 90 degrees. The guides informed us that we would climb up that wall. I was thinking, "I'm not going up that damn wall, impossible, how could I climb a 1,000 foot vertical face, no way in hell!"

As darkness fell we had dinner of a warm meat and vegetable stew while we sat around a small fire. At that altitude there was a shortage of firewood. My fellow climbers seemed much more serious about mountain climbing than I was. Face it, I was here because Vicki read a book. The others talked about other climbs and were there to reach the summit. I thought it was a pretty cool place and kept asking the guides questions about trails that we crossed and what's that? And where does this go? By the second day they ignored my questions and marched on. The night we camped at this wall there was a full moon. The rest of the group went to their tents after dinner. I sat out there watching clouds that magically formed, covered the moon, then dissipated. The sky would be clear for a little while, then a cloud would form again, then disappear, over and over again. For a while another climber from Salt Lake City watched the moon and cloud show, then he went to his tent. I wasn't sleepy, an effect of altitude perhaps.

Morning came and we prepared to assault the impossible breach wall. Carved into the rock was a very narrow vertical switchback trail. We all had hiking poles, and as we ascended I had to balance carefully without looking down. By noon we climbed off the wall and hiked over a series of hills ranging from 13,500 feet to 14,000 feet, up and down. After about five hours of this we faced uphill for the final 1,500 foot climb for the day. I lost my appetite, forgot to drink water, lagged behind, and wondered if I could make it to the next camp. By this time, the group was strung out into a long line of hikers. I was one of three laggards at the end, the other two were behind me. About dark I trudged into the camp. This camp actually had an outhouse. It stood on a steep edge of the mountain and when you entered it, it tipped back and forth. I wondered if it might just slip down the mountain. At this altitude vomiting and diarrhea are common, and the outhouse had an indescribable stench. Luckily I avoided the vomiting and diarrhea, but I was dehydrated and lacked energy. I tried drinking as much as I could and ate what I was able to choke down. The plan for the next morning was to leave at 2 a.m. and climb to the top. Four thousand feet more! It was critical to leave hours before sunrise because the top of the mountain is scree, small rocks that slide all over the place when you step on them. Before the sunrise the scree is frozen and it's easier to get a steady foothold.

Shortly before 2 a.m. the camp stirred. I woke up feeling great. Two other people were feeling sick from the extreme altitude and would begin the descent. Suddenly I decided to join the sickies and not go for the summit. Why did I make that decision? Somewhere in my mind I realized how stupid this belt-notching, summit achievement attitude was. When you reach an altitude that no longer can support life, isn't it foolish just to defy that for the sake of your ego? Again, why was I there? I would have liked to explore the mountain where life did exist. And of course there is the aspect of fear, testing the unknown. What is the point? Getting up at 2 a.m. just to climb a mountain where half the group will be vomiting and miserable didn't get my vote. So we three laggards got up with the sun and followed one of the porters to another trail to begin the descent.

Now we were on the "tourist" trail. If a climber just showed up at the bottom of the mountain this would be the trail that one would take. It was a deeply worn path, four to five feet wide. This trail was easy, there were no breach walls to contend with. We reached the camp where we would be spending the night. This camp had running water (very cold), toilets and a café and bar. There were permanent buildings set up dormitory style. Here climbers from all over the world created a party atmosphere. In retrospect, this would have been a more enjoyable way to see the mountain. Around dark the tired looking group that had hiked to the top showed up in camp. Tales of exaltation and vomiting ensued. That evening a heavy mist fell. When I woke up in my tiny blue tent I tried to unzip myself out of there to use an almost real toilet, but the zippers were frozen solid. I had to wait for the sun to hit the tent to escape. I began to laugh. Frozen in a tent at 12,000 feet would be a good start to a horror story or maybe a silly comedy. Once the sun hit the tent the ice melted quickly. This was the last day at Kilimanjaro, it was downhill from there.

It took a challenge like this mountain climbing experience to go into my psyche to understand what kind of a person I am. Unchallenged, I lack the motivation for self-examination. Now I could see it was exploration that I enjoyed. Reaching the top of the mountain would have been a good boasting topic. But I really didn't give a damn about the top of the mountain. I wanted to see the place. Maybe I wanted to make up for all the unusual places I had gone to but had never taken the time off from the work to explore. Often I had climbed around the Sierras on the small trails off the Pacific Crest trail looking for blooming flowers, hidden lakes, and oddball trees. At the age of 55 I could accept this was who I was.

- Lesson twenty-nine: If I knew then what I know now about climbing Kilimanjaro, I would have gone independent of the prearranged trip and hired my own guide to go up the tourist trail. I would have explored the more interesting places below the tree line where life exists.

## Chapter 20 - ICA Congress in Brazil

May 13, 1997--Visa date for Brazil

Brazil hosted the 1997 ICA Congress to be held in Belo Horizonte. Sydney agreed to help with the auction and we arrived in Rio a few days before we had to be in Belo. We found a hotel with a beach view. Now I could be a real tourist. Late one evening we walked on the beautiful black and white walkway bordering Copacabana Beach without getting mugged — this was not recommended by the locals. "Winter" in Brazil seemed to be fairly quiet. The tram ride up to Sugar Loaf overlooks the aquamarine bay and the entire city. High-rise buildings shield the view of the rampant slums. Of course, no trip to Rio is complete without a tour up to the Christ the Redeemer statue. This time all the shrines and voodoo stuff had been removed a few days before a visit from the Pope. Unlike my usual hit-and-run business trips, we had time to visit the tourist shops.

A new Belo Horizonte replaced what I had visited in 1979. The hotel, without suicide showers, was close to a small strip mall shopping center featuring Burger King and McDonald's. For that we could have stayed home. What is the world coming to? Tim Roark was the ICA auction chairman. Among the Brazilians on the host auction committee was an emerald dealer, Luis Martins, who owned a couple of emerald mines in Brazil. Also one of the committee members was a close associate of Hans Stern who had arrived in Brazil as a young adolescent and was one of the "children of the Kristallnacht." Together they had gone door to door selling gemstones. Eventually Stern had saved enough money to open up a retail gem and jewelry store. This developed into a worldwide business, H. Stern. Brazil, like the United States, is a country with a variety of immigrants. Perhaps the new blood flowing into new world countries stimulates the buccaneer spirit proliferating in the gem business. Luis escorted Sydney to some of the evening outings for the Congress. (He was a few years younger than I am). Sydney was the chief typist for this auction, so I was freed to help out with the rest of the production.

This conference had evening extravanzas out of the hotel. One evening we took a long bus ride and ended up in the country by a lake with picnic facilities. We arrived before dark for the cocktail hour. As the sun set, the band showed up. One of the speakers was about twelve feet high and blasted out sound I found physically painful. When the musicians arrived and began to play, the music blared out at some horrible decibel level. I had to leave. Sydney could hang out with Tim for the evening. And I left, walking down a road somewhere in the world--I had no idea where I was. Escape from the painful sound was all I could think about. Where was I going? I wandered onto the main road. Within five minutes a taxi came by. I waved him down and asked him to take me to the hotel. Fifteen minutes later I was at the hotel. It had taken the bus an hour to take us out. In retrospect, what was I thinking to leave and wander off when I had no idea where I was? How many taxis were out there that night?

After the Congress, Luis invited Sydney to visit one of his emerald mines located in Nova Era, about an hour from Belo. I wasn't on his guest list, so I had to beg him to go. Sydney really didn't care about emerald mines, but I wanted every gem experience I could find. The emerald deposit was about 150 feet underground. Entry into the mine entailed hanging onto a sturdy wire line that was raised and lowered into the mine. Tough, muscular young miners would grab onto the wire with their hands and go underground. So for me to descend I had to hold on to a miner. Fun! For the first fifty feet going down there was faint light. For the next fifty feet we were sprayed with mist, signifying we had entered the underground water level. Having adequate water pumps to remove the water in these underground mines was essential to the safety of the miners. The last fifty feet were in total darkness. We landed on a flat quartz surface and entered a cavern with large lamps lighting the mica-coated space. Mica forms in thin layered sheets adhered together into small bundles of sparkly stone which becomes powdered when disturbed. It is used in makeup to give it a glittery, shiny look. The whole cavern glittered. Crawling around the mine my clothes became covered with mica. Oh, yes, there were emeralds somewhere embedded in the walls of the cavern. Meanwhile there was dynamite blasting in another mine located about a hundred yards away. The sound of the blasts was somewhat muted, but still sounded ominous. Mild tremors could be felt. I found it pretty exciting. When we ascended from the mine about a half-hour later Sydney folded up into a fearful little ball. She didn't experience the same exhilaration that I did.

Luis said that I could go down into the neighboring mine. Of course I went. Once again I leapt into darkness with a cute muscular miner. At the entrance to the mine cavern was a downward slanted runway carved out of solid white quartz. Water was running down the quartz slide. I had to sit down in the water to enter the mine. Even though I was wet, I burst out laughing--it reminded me of the Pirates of the Caribbean ride at Disneyland. This was the ultimate thrill for me, much better than Disneyland.

Of course all this fun had to end. On the way back to the hotel Luis looked at me and said in a critical manner, "I know what you are, you're an adventurer."This was no compliment coming from him. I don't know whether that was a form of criticism or merely a fact. Yes, absolutely, he had defined me in a way that I hadn't thought about. I guess I'm no different from the other buccaneers out there looking for the new thrills and experiences that are out of the mainstream. He defined me very well.

The auction didn't make any money for ICA and this was the last one. It was also the last ICA Congress that I would attend. Sometimes outside forces sweep us into new territory. A tidal wave of responsibility seemed to hit me at home and I soon evolved into a new life.

- Lesson thirty: After twenty years of all these exciting adventures, it was time to move on. Living on the edge can get tiring.

## Chapter 21 - L.A. MAN!

March, 2013 — Los Angeles, California

After escaping from Los Angeles in 1970, I've had little interest in returning. My last visit was in the late 1990s when I helped my friend Nancy move there to be closer to her daughter. Now it was time for a return visit. A client had given me an expensive yellow sapphire to have made into a fantastic piece of jewelry. The master jeweler I use lives in North Hollywood, and I decided to hand-deliver the stone. At the same time I could visit Nancy.

I was ready for a little bit of L.A. nostalgia. Nancy lived a block below Sunset Boulevard in West Hollywood in a beautiful tree-shaded neighborhood with 1920s Art Deco apartments. Incessant bird serenades masked the discordant traffic noise in this peaceful pocket hidden in the city of chaos.

On Sunday, March 17, 2013, the Los Angeles Marathon raced through this section of Sunset Boulevard--the midpoint of the race. About 8:30 that morning I walked up to Sunset to give Nancy some time to do whatever she needed to take care of. People lined the Boulevard cheering on the runners. The first few runners I saw were all men, shirtless, extremely fit, perfectly pec'd, seemingly oblivious to the sidewalk observers. These included some of the world's best marathoners. A few minutes later a couple of women ran by. As time passed the runners grew into a rainbow of racers of all nationalities, body types, abilities, and ages. Then there were a few participants who had begun to walk at this midway point. The runners in these later groups appeared to be having a good time: they knew they weren't going to win the marathon. As these runners passed by, the mood became more celebratory — a Mardi Gras-like atmosphere without the beads. Having fun seemed to be their reason to be out on this foggy Sunday morning. Green t-shirts dominated the clothing worn — it was St. Patrick's Day. One runner was barefoot, a few wore silly costumes. The sidewalk crowd clapped as runners passed. Some observers held signs encouraging their friends to keep running.

By 10:00 a.m. I realized this was a metaphor of life. There are those who train and prepare to go the distance. The competitive Type-A personalities are serious about winning or getting a good time to satisfy their egos. For some it could make them celebrities. A Kenyan man, Erick Mose, won this marathon in 2 hours and 9 minutes. Aleksandra Duliba from Belarus won the women's portion in 2 hours and 26 minutes. National heroes!

Most of the runners are there however, with their personal goals, searching for their sense of accomplishment. For me, my life's adventures are about exploration and experience. My only regret about going to Kilimanjaro is that I didn't have the opportunity to explore the forest areas more. On my international trips, I always enjoyed my early morning forays on the streets before the business day started, those normally quiet times when you could walk around without the distraction of lots of people and traffic. Those walks gave me a sense of inner peace, time to solve problems and plan my day.

We can choose to participate, seriously to win, or to simply enjoy the experience, or we can sit at home. What have I done with my life? I have chosen the experience, which was implemented by the chance of meeting the right people at the right time. That was pure luck or maybe a divine plan. Who knows if we all have a preplanned destiny? I was blind to the possibility of failure, but reached some success, and survived a few rough spots along the way.

Today I avoid airports and prefer dirt roads that lead to mysterious slot canyons in Utah or petroglyph sites a few minutes away from my neighborhood in Arizona. It really is about the journey — and the French fries........

# TECHNICAL GEM FACTS

Beryl: Beryl is a complex mineral that includes brilliant green emeralds, aquamarines, as well as golden beryl, morganite and bixbite. Hardness of beryls is 7.

Aquamarine is a watery blue beryl as the name implies. The colors range from a light to medium blue or a greenish blue. Often the rough gem material comes out of the mine with greenish tints; then it is heated to produce a bluer stone. Darker blues are hard to find and some darker material has visible inclusions. Fine rutile needle inclusions can produce aquamarine cat's eyes.

Bixbite has an intense red color. This very rare stone is mined in Utah.

Emerald is the intense green form of beryl. Chromium and small amounts vanadium and iron create the intense green color in emeralds. Green beryls without the chromium are not considered emeralds.

Golden beryl is the yellow variety.

Morganite is the pink variety and was named after banker, J. P. Morgan.

Andalusite: Andalusite is highly dichroic—it shows three different colors that emanate from three different axes within the gem crystal. Red, green, and yellow comprise the colors of better quality andalusite. When looking at andalusite the human eye mixes the colors into a brownish appearing stone.

Hardness is 7 ½, a reasonable hardness for jewelry use.

<u>Corundum</u>: Rubies and sapphires are composed of aluminum oxide. They have a hardness of 9, making them tough and durable. The most valuable stones have intense color and no distracting inclusions.

Rubies are the red variety of corundum. By a gemologist's interpretation this means red-red. But the line between pink sapphire and ruby is ambiguous. If the stone are pale or purplish, they are "pink sapphires."Rubies are mined commercially in Thailand, Mozambique, Madagascar, Burma, and Vietnam. Political issues may affect the availability of rubies from Burma and Vietnam. If rubies have not been "burned" in the rough stage, the inclusions are helpful in determining the origin of the stone. Burning dissolves any rutile in the stone and intensifies the color and is a routine treatment.

Sapphires include all the other colors of corundum other than red-red: blue, green, yellow, pink, orange, violet, brown and black. Blue is the most sought after color, along with ones that are distinctly pink. Thai blue sapphires tend to be dark blue with blackish overtones. Sri Lanka produces sapphires with vibrant blue colors and are most available commercially. Rumor has it that sapphires from Kashmir are the best, but looking for one is like going on a snipe hunt. The mine is located in the northwest portion of the Himalayas at an elevation of nearly 15,000 feet which is covered in snow most of the year. Green sapphires are abundant in Thailand, but their "army green" color holds little appeal. Other colors are less available. Violet sapphires (mostly from Sri Lanka) may be the most overlooked sapphire treasure. Star rubies and sapphires come in a variety of colors. Asterism (stars) occurs when the corundum is included with rutile needles.

Feldspars: A group of minerals with similar chemical compositions and varying crystal forms.

Moonstones constitute the most important feldspar gems. They form in various colors: semi-translucent yellow, orange, greens, grays and whites are found in India. Some have needle-like inclusions that produce chatoyancy. Most treasured are blue flash moonstones. The blue flash is created by thin internal layering creating an optical interference that appears as a blue flash.

Sunstones include a range of gems. These sunstones are found with a range of body colors ranging from pink to oranges, tans, greens, and rarely red stones. Traces of hematite and copper inclusions create the schiller (sparkling) effect. India produces many sunstones with an orange-brown schiller in a colorless body color. Beautiful green and red sunstones are mined in Oregon.

233

Labradorite is a gray bodied gem with brilliant flashes of blues, greens, golds, and reds. The schiller in labradorite is created by layers of twinned crystals and needle-like inclusions. Labradorite found in Finland is called "spectrolite."

Garnets: Although garnets are usually thought of as red stones, there are many varieties with vibrant colors. A group of similar chemical compounds compose the garnet family. Garnets are fairly hard, ranging from 7 ¼ to 7 ½ on Moh's scale. Each group in the family differs slightly in its refractive index.

Almandine garnets are the most common dark red garnets. Darker stones absorb most of the light and less brilliance is reflected out.

Pyrope garnets are blood red to brownish red. Some small brilliant red ones are mined in Arizona; these are referred to as "ant hill" garnets.

Rhodolite garnets fall somewhere between almandines and pyropes chemically and optically. They range in color from dark violetish red to a pinkish red. Lighter pink ones can have the "wow" factor.

Spessarite garnets range from orange to brownish red colors. They have higher refractive indexes and are quite brilliant. Some of the spectacular orange ones fall into the "wow" group.

Grossular garnets are found in a variety of colors: pinks, yellow, browns and greens. Grossulars can form in transparent crystals as well as massive material that is semi-opaque. Tsavorites fall in the grossular group and fine ones are definitely "wow" stones. Spectacular oranges and pinks can also hit the "wow" meter if you are lucky enough to find one.

Andradite garnets have the highest refractive index in the group—they are rare and usually quite small. Colors range from yellowish brown to brown.

Demantoid garnets are rare and can be the most spectacular of the garnet group. A good one has a brilliant green color with exceptional dispersion.

Few garnets occur purely in one group or another. Most have atoms that dominate another group. One time I asked Fred Pough what to call garnets that fall in between groups. He replied, "Garnet! "

Jades: Nephrite and jadeite are both called "jade."Appearance-wise and optically these two are somewhat similar.

Nephrite jade was treasured by the ancient Chinese. It is the toughest of gemstones due to its fibrous structure, although its hardness is only 6 1/2. It is found in white and dark green colors. Nephrite was carved into amulets symbolizing various spiritual beliefs. It was also carved into celts that could easy break a skull.

Jadeite is the more expensive of the jades. Its hardness is 7. Gray, light brown, yellow and pale greens are the most common jadeite colors, but intense rich green material and dark lavender color are rare and the most valuable. Jadeite from Burma was discovered in the 1700's. The finest green jadeite with translucence is called "Imperial jade." Another ancient source of rich green jadeite is in Guatemala. The Mayans carved this jade into human figured amulets only to be worn by royalty. Coincidently around 1000 B. C.in Costa Rica jadeite was carved into celts that are very similar to the Chinese nephrite celts.

Lapis Lazuli: Lapis lazuli is a rock comprised of sodalite, calcite, and pyrite. The best quality is mined in Afghanistan.

Opal: Opals come in transparent and opaque varieties. Some of the transparent varieties with body colors of white, black, yellows, orange, red and colorless show a "play of color."Yellow, orange, and red stones are called "fire opals;" they may or may not show a "play of color."Opaque varieties form in yellow, pink and blue colors. Opal can form into the cells of wood or into seashells creating opalized fossils.

The structure of an opal is a hardened jelly, basically a gel. Chemically it consists of $SiO_2$ and water. It does not crystallize in a consistent manner. It is fragile and brittle in character.

Hardness of opal ranges from 5 ½ to 6 ½.

Pearls: Mollusks, abalone, conch, oysters, mussels, clams, cowries and others, create pearls when irritants inhabit them. Pearls are essentially nature's way of creating a "scab" around a grain of sand or small worm that penetrates the shell of a mollusk.

**Cultured pearls** were developed in Japan in the 1890's by Kokichi Mikimoto. He took Akoya oysters and surgically inserted a mother of pearl beads. The oysters are then put into mesh bags and placed in the ocean for a couple of years. "Nacre" grows around the bead giving the bead its "pearly luster."

**South Sea pearls** were found naturally and then cultured in Tahiti, Australia, and Indonesia. Pearls found around Tahiti grow in the black lipped oyster, *pinctada marfaritifera*, and have near black body colors, silvery grays, or darker body colors. Around Australia and Indonesia silver lipped oysters, *pinctada maxima*, create white to golden colored pearls as well as an occasional pastel color. The color of the interior layer inside a shell determines the ultimate color of the pearl.

**Freshwater pearls** grow in mollusks in fresh water sources--lakes and rivers. Freshwater pearls found in the rivers of Europe and the British Isles were used in jewelry for at least two thousand years. Culturing of the fresh water mussels was first done in Lake Biwa in Japan. Commercial freshwater pearls are grown in Chinese rivers and in the Mississippi Valley. Freshwater pearls form in a variety of colors — white, pinks, golds, lavenders, and peach. Shapes of freshwater pearls are varied and are determined by the shape of the tissue inserted into the pearl.

**Keishi** pearls are non-nucleated pearls, in other words they don't have a bead center. These pearls have formed around of a bit of the mollusk's flesh that was used to insert the bead into the mollusk. Keishi pearls have unusual shapes and often an exceptional luster.

Peridot: A yellow-green gemstone with a hardness of 6 ½. Large peridot are found in Burma. Smaller stones are mined in the San Carlos reservation in Arizona. They are also mined in China.

Quartz: The quartz family, silicon dioxide, includes an interesting variety of gem materials. Pure quartz is transparent and colorless. Under the right geologic conditions it can form into very large crystals. Mineral impurities give creates quartz gems: amethyst, citrine, ametrine, and rose quartz. Citrine, yellow quartz, is quite rare in nature; commercial quantities are a result of heating amethyst. Ametrine, which occurs naturally is a bicolored stone consisting of amethyst and citrine.

Inclusions in crystalline quartz create fascinating gems. Rutillated quartz has golden to orange colored needles that form into varied patterns. Black tourmaline crystals form in "tourmalinated quartz."Minute rutile needles form six rayed stars in "star rose quartz."

Chalcedony is composed of tiny fibrous quartz crystal fibers. Stones range from translucent to opaque. Gem quality chalcedonies include pastel blue, pink, lavender, green (chrysoprase), and orange (carnelian). Banded chalcedonies are referred to as agates. The Romans began dyeing banded chalcedonies to carve into cameos.

Jasper has an even smaller quartz crystalline structure and is opaque. Jaspers form in many earthy colors: browns, yellows, brownish reds, and green. It takes a good polish. Jasper has been carved for millennia into amulets, stamp seals, and jewelry stones. Some multicolored jaspers can look like miniature landscapes.

Sodalite: Sodalite has an opaque deep royal blue color. It resembles lapis lazuli because it is a component of lapis lazuli. But lapis lazuli is a "rock" comprised of a mixture of sodalite, pyrite and calcite.

Sodalite has a hardness of 5 ½ to 6.

Spinel: Spinel are found in brilliant reds, hot pinks, pastel pinks, grays, oranges , blues and violets. Hardness is 8. Sources are Burma, Sri Lanka, and Afganistan.

Tourmaline: Tourmaline has a complex chemical composition and is found in a full color spectrum of hues and range from pastels to darker colors. Different deposits around the world produce various colors created by the trace minerals present, so each source has distinctive features. Chrome bearing tourmalines mined in Africa have an intense green color not found in Brazilian green tourmaline. Gem quality tourmalines are usually eye clean except for the pinkish red stones, rubellite (red), and bicolors, which are often quite included. Tourmalines with fibrous inclusions produce cat's eyes. Finer quality tourmalines are generally faceted. Multicolor crystals can be cut into "slices." Lesser qualities can be cut into cabochons.

Tourmaline have a hardness ranging from 7 to 7 ½. They are not particularly brittle.

Topaz: Topaz occurs in nature as brown, yellow, orange, pink, red, colorless, and pale blue, mostly pastel tones. Some brown topaz crystals can turn to an intense orange or strawberry red color when heated. The near red ones are quite rare and the most pricey of the topazes. Some colorless topaz can be irradiated, then heated to turn into intense blue colors. Blue topaz used in jewelry is most often the irradiated and heated material.

Topaz has a hardness of 8.

Zircon: Natural zircons occur in earthy colors of browns, red, orange, yellow and green. These colors are rarely found set into jewelry. With heat treatment, some zircons turn colorless or a brilliant medium blue color. Hardness is 7. Zircon has a high refractive index giving it an exceptional brilliance. The colorless and blue stone are used in jewelry, but they abrade easily. Burma and Cambodia are major sources of zircon.

# CRYSTAL SYSTEMS

Most gemstones are crystallized minerals. A crystal forms with atoms fixed into a defined symmetrical pattern. There are seven crystal systems that have from two to four axes. (Imagine an axis as a plane inside the crystal.) Crystal axes vary in length.

Cubic system: In this system there are two axes with the same length that are perpendicular to each other. Diamonds, garnets, and spinel form into cubic crystals.

Tetragonal system: There are three axes in this system. The horizontal has two axes of the same length that are perpendicular to each other. The lengthwise axis is a different length from the horizontal axes; it may be shorter or longer. Zircons and rutile have tetragonal systems.

Orthorhombic system: Three axes run at right angles to each other in this system. All axes have a different length. Common gems that form in the orthorhombic system are peridot, chrysoberyl, topaz, andalusite, and iolite.

Monoclinic system: This system has three axes, each with a different length. Two of the axes form at right angles, the third runs at an oblique angle to the others. Orthoclase feldspars, kunzite, and sphene all have form in the monoclinic system.

<u>Triclinic system:</u> There are three axes of unequal lengths that do not have right angles to each other in this system. Turquoise and plagioclase feldspars form in the triclinic systems.

<u>Hexagonal system</u>: Hexagonal crystals have four axes; three axes of equal length are at 60 degree angles to each other on the horizontal plane. The fourth axis has a right angle running through the center of the three other axes and is either shorter or longer that the other three axes. Basically a hexagonal pattern is formed with the three axes. Beryls and apatite fall into this system.

<u>Trigonal (rhombohedral) system</u>: Like the hexagonal system, this system has four axes with similar relationships. This system has a more triangular symmetry, rather than a six sided arrangement. Tourmaline, corundum (rubies and sapphires), and quartz fall into this system.

PLEASE NOTE: Some gemologist advocate for six crystal systems by combining the hexagonal and trigonal systems together. At the Gemological Institute of America (GIA), I learned the six systems. Europeans seem to prefer the seven systems. Also note that the Brits spell gemmological with two "m's".

# GEMSTONE TREATMENT (Partial list)

Heating: This is the most common treatment. Heating can lighten or alter the color of certain gems: tourmaline, topaz, aquamarine, amethyst, rubies and sapphires. Commercial citrine comes from heated amethyst. Heating can also burn out inclusions in some gems, especially rubies and sapphires.

Dyeing: Porous gem materials can absorb dyes. The ancient Romans dyed gray agate into black onyx which does not occur in nature. Turquoise can be dyed. Jadeite can be dyed a dark emerald green or medium lavender color: this treatment is difficult to detect.

Irradiation: Various forms of nuclear bombardment can alter certain gemstone's color. Diamonds can be irradiated and heated to create blues, greens, yellows and rarely other colors. Commercial blue topaz has been irradiated and heated. Natural blue topaz exists, but it has a pale insipid color.

Oiling: Colorless materials can fill surface cracks to improve the gem's appearance.

Lasering: Use of a laser to "burn" out an inclusion (mainly used for diamonds).

Impregation: Porous gemstones can be filled with colorless materials, thus improving its durability. This often done to turquoise — it darkens the color a bit and protects it from absorbing substances that could eventually discolor the turquoise.

# APPENDIX

GEMOLOGICAL GEOLOGY: Rocks cover much of the earth's surface. "Rock" is created by various minerals combining into an aggregate. With a few exceptions gem materials are "pure minerals."Rocks and minerals are classified into igneous, sedimentary, or metamorphic. All of these processes create gem materials.

Igneous rocks come from molten magma from under the earth's surface; they surface through volcanic action or come up through fissures in the earth's crust.

Sedimentary rocks are created by combinations of erosion—wind, water, and/or ice.

Metamorphic rock forms when igneous or sedimentary rocks are subjected to heat and pressure somewhere in the earth's crust. A transformation of the rock occurs and new minerals are formed.

Brazil, Sri Lanka, Burma/Thailand, and Madagascar are areas especially blessed by extensive gem deposits.

Pegmatites form from igneous rock and can produce fairly large crystals. Basic pegmatite consists of quartz and feldspar and can contain crystals of tourmaline, beryl, garnet, and topaz. Mining this hard rock challenges the miner to remove the stones without breaking the crystals. These deposits may be mined by cutting away the hillside to get the stones or creating underground shafts into the pegmatites to remove the gemmy material. Mines that go deep into the ground require more difficult processes for extraction. Where ground water is high, water must be continually pumped out. Cave-ins occur, making mining dangerous and hard work.

Sedimentary deposits can contain gem bearing gravels known as alluvials. These form in ancient river beds. Gems from these deposits are found as water worn pebbles. In primitive areas gemmy material is panned like gold.

Some gems are dug out of soil deposits. This dry digging process can be mechanized by placing soils on a sluiceway and washing away the soil with water, thus leaving behind the heavier gem materials.

Rough is the term for gem materials as they are removed from the ground.

# GLOSSARY

<u>Adularescence</u>: refers to the internal flashes of color in moonstones.

<u>Asterism</u>: refers to star formations in gemstones.

<u>Brilliance</u>: refers to the ability of a gemstone to reflect light to the viewer. The refractive index determines the potential brilliance, but the clarity, cutting proportions, and polish will influence the overall brilliance of a finished stone.

<u>Cabochon</u>: unfaceted stones with polished tops and bottoms. Most often a cabochon will have a rounded top and flat bottom.

<u>Calibrated stones</u>: stones cut to standard millimeter sizes. For example: 2, 3, 4, 5 mm, rounds; 5X3, 6X4, 7X5 mm. ovals and so forth.

<u>Chatoyancy</u>: describes the "eye" visible in some gemstones.

<u>Cleavage</u>: the direction of weakness within a stone to break along certain internal planes within the stones.

<u>Culet</u>: the tiny facet on the bottom of a faceted gemstone.

<u>Dispersion</u>: the spectral display given off by some gemstones. Diamonds, sphene, and demantoid garnets are especially dispersive.

<u>Face up</u>: when a gemstone is viewed looking down onto the table. This is how the gem would appear when set.

Turning the gem table side down, it may be possible to see color zoning and possible some larger inclusions.

Facet: the polished geometric portion of a gemstone.

Flaws: describes unattractive inclusions.

Hardness: refers to the scratchability of a material, i.e. a harder material will scratch a softer material. For gemstones this is measured by the Moh's scale.

Inclusions: this describes the internal landscape of a gemstone. On the positive side: the inclusions can define the origin of a gem. They can determine if the gem is found in nature or if it is a synthetic. On the negative side: eye visible inclusions can detract from the beauty of a gem. "Flaws" also describes detracting inclusions.

Luster: refers to the surface brilliance of a gem. The luster of a stone depends on its hardness and quality of polishing. A pearls luster is created by layers of its nacre.

Moh's Scale: a number is assigned to each gem material to define its hardness. 1. Talc, 2. Gypsum, 3. Calcite, 4. Apatite, 5. Fluorite, 6. Orthoclase feldspar, 7. Quartz, 8. Topaz, 9. Corundum, 10. Diamond.

Nacre: layers of crystalline calcium carbonate that form around a pearl's nucleus giving it the lustrous pearly look.

Phenomenal: refers to gemstones with interesting visual effects: asterism, adularescence, chatoyancy, and schiller.

 Play of color: flashes of color emanating from a transparent opal.

<u>Pleochroism and dicroism</u>: gemstones with different internal axis lengths absorb light at different rates. This means different colors can be emitted from each axis. This may affect the apparent color of a stone. As you turn certain stones around you may see different colors. Dichroism refers to those stones which might emit two colors. Pleochroism refers to those which show three colors.

<u>Refractive index</u>: refers to the ability of a stone to bend light internally. Generally, the refractive index predicts the "brilliance" of a stone.

<u>Rough</u>: refers to gem material as it has been removed from the ground. (Before cutting and polishing.)

<u>Schiller</u>: describes the internal shimmer in sunstones.

<u>Table</u>: the top facet on a faceted gemstone.

<u>Toughness</u>: Although hardness is a factor in how tough a gemstone is, internal structure also affects the durability and toughness of a gemstone.

## About the Author

Sondra Francis trained to become a graduate gemologist from the Gemological Institute of America, experiencing her passion for gemstones in a very exciting way. In retirement she leads a busy life as a glass artist in Arizona.

32295742R00147

Made in the USA
San Bernardino, CA
02 April 2016